Bo!

my brother in it. Christ - Oh my, but its probably a good thing we didn't meet in 1960. (Smile). Love you my bro

[signature]

Aug 16. 2019

M000099736

CORONADO CONFIDENTIAL

"It Can't Happen Here . . ."

— JOE DITLER —

Coronado Confidential: It Can't Happen Here

ISBN: 978-1-7320962-3-3 (hardcover)

Library of Congress Control Number: 2019905775

Printed in the United States of America

This book is dedicated to Jack and Chelsea.
I hope you remember to do what I say, not what I did.
I love you, and I'm so very, very proud of you.

CONTENTS

FOREWORD

From obscure little Muscoy in Southern California's Inland Empire to the seemingly sleepy island of Coronado, an unlikely milieu of retired admirals and aging hippies, fringed with palm trees angled and shaped by the wind, Joe Ditler stirs the cobwebs of those who shared his fondness and folly for the highs and lows of the Sixties.

Told by a master storyteller, his phantasmagorical tales tell of an unforgettable era that thrived in an even unlikelier place.

One can't help but be awestruck, dumbstruck even, by the self-induced twists and turns of his curious and often uproarious life as a teen-ager and beyond. That was Joe. Still is. Except he's not so young anymore.

The Sixties Revolution erupted all over the world, but nowhere near to the degree it did on the West Coast of California, from San Francisco's Haight-Ashbury hippie mecca all the way to Coronado, San Diego's deceptively quaint, conservative military enclave across the bay. Hard to believe, even now.

Sixties miscreant minstrel Frank Zappa put it this way: "It can't happen here." But it did.

Deftly and soulfully, Joe Ditler reawakens the memories, music, and madness of a half-century-ago generation that left an undeniably lasting imprint on today's culture and lifestyle. He was there, and now he's here, to tell his story. . .

I didn't know Joe back then, but as a long-time friend and fellow writer—a storytelling peer in the truest definition, I'm certain he didn't make any of this crazy s--- up, even the craziest. Nobody could.

If Joe says it happened, I believe him. I just can't believe he's still here to write so deliciously about the mischief and lunacy of that time long ago that left a lasting imprint on who we are today.

This is a read you will long savor and not soon forget.

— John Freeman, journalist/author, and former columnist
for the *San Diego Union-Tribune* newspaper.

INTRODUCTION

Ever since I was a kid in school
I messed around with all the rules
Apologized, then realized
I'm not different after all.

—Rod Stewart

People ask what I do for a living. That could be a long story, but I've learned to just explain that, years ago, I chose passion over paycheck. I suppose that's about as good an explanation as one could come up with, having been a writer for the past half century.

And yet, as a writer, I've found myself discovering the world through the lives of others. I've worked so many, many facets of this industry. I've been writer and photographer, caption writer and advertising salesman, editor and publisher, author, freelancer, ghost writer and collaborator. I've done articles, biographies, press releases, books, speeches and even obituaries.

The latter has turned into quite a surprise little business, especially when I put the more progressive spin on it by suggesting people allow me to do their story, their "living obituary," before they die. It's all storytelling in one way or another, the preserving of someone's story, or recalling something from our past.

I've eulogized celebrities and old schooners, admirals and recluses, and even dogs and cats. I've done too many to count, but every so often someone asks, "Hey, have you done your own?"

Home (above and below) is where your wagon wheel is. This is 2233 First Street, Muscoy. My dad called it, "Hell's Half Acre." It was home to three Ditlers, two horses, cows, sheep and goats, dogs, pigeons, turtles and snakes.

My obituary? Nah. No time to write such a thing. Too busy living to die anyway.

I tried once to write it, and what should have been an 800-word document turned quickly into 6,000 words, and I was just getting started. While I may not have penned my obit, I've hired the entertainment for my wake.

I cut deals with bagpipers, folk-rock performers, torch singers and the like, that, if I died before them, they would play at my wake. If they died first, or so went our verbal covenant, I'd write the most beautiful tribute

to them the world has ever seen. Well, I think most of them have forgotten our deal.

I'd be pleased to hear Ron's Garage Band, Gonzology, or the West Coast Ironworks playing as I dance my way up to Heaven because they, above all others, capture the special music of my youth. But enough of that. I've got plenty to do before that time comes.

Jobs? I've had so many damned job titles it makes me dizzy just trying to remember them all. I've managed major museums and non-profits on both sides of the bridge. I've raised millions of dollars for charities.

Muscoy wasn't without its benefits. Taffy was a regal Palomino and one of three horses I rode as a child.

I drove Hertz rent-a-cars back and forth from Los Angeles to San Diego, delivered pizzas for Joey's Italian Eatery, waited tables at a myriad of restaurants—the Rib Cage, Krishna Mulvaney's, Brigantine, Le Onion, McP's.

I taught SCUBA diving and made underwater camera lenses. I schlepped cement for Bud "The Batman" Bernhard, taught yoga at a local college and tennis at the Hotel del Coronado. I've cleaned bathrooms, pumped gas, sold pot and painted houses. The list goes on . . .

And then there is the writing and public relations. My early writing career was centered around sports. I co-owned a tennis and racquetball monthly newspaper, as well as the official fan publications for the San

Diego Clippers and San Francisco Giants. "Co-owned" meant I had to do everything—interviews, writing, editing, photographing, darkroom work, ad sales, etc.

I conceptualized the red-carpet movie premier for 20th Century Fox and the film *Master & Commander*, hosted a movie premier on board the tallship Star of India for the movie *Cutthroat Island*, and worked special projects with the likes of Charlton Heston and Jane Russell.

By the mid-'80s I had become an internationally known waterfront writer, with work published throughout the United States, England, Australia and New Zealand. During the America's Cup, I owned and operated a news-clipping service.

I remain the obit writer who can't even pen his own obituary. But, if someone can't engrave a pretty thorough obit from all of this, then let's not even bother. "Tomb of the Unknown Writer" might be a fitting epitaph.

When I'm gone, I'd be happy with a wooden bench facing the Shipwreck along Coronado's southern shores. Perhaps add a small plaque with my name and appropriate sentiment. I think it would be nice for old friends and family to go there at times and think of me.

***

The idea of writing a book about growing up in Coronado has long been in the back of my mind.

For the past several years, I've used Facebook as a form of relaxation—a place where I can write something that no one pays me for, where no editor can edit or mark up my copy, or shave off 100 words because it's too long. For me, it's a place where there are no deadlines.

Sometimes I do so even at the expense of work I need to get done. I know. My bad. But being able to write free-form like that, much of it from memories or inspired by the odd historical document or photograph I have run across over the years, well, it's like a medicine for me. It tends to lubricate the creative muscles of my mind—and that's a good thing.

Our backyard in Muscoy was often the scene of gatherings such as this. My dad was a Big Band trumpet player. He kept his lip intact through the 1950s alternating between band gigs and work as a TV repairman. That's me, being fondled by the Khyber girls from up the street. Photo by Esther Ditler.

I've found it to be an addictive and pleasant place to play, like a big eSandbox for old guys and frustrated writers.

Sometimes, I'm late on two or three real-life deadlines, and I just want to throw my hands in the air, sit back and recall a memory from my youth—usually something terribly embarrassing and self-deprecating. You know, the type of stuff you really don't want your kids to know about. The stuff they end up finding out about anyway.

The result of all those little stories, anecdotes and memories has been a small army of friends and followers insisting I write a book. Thank you to all my many friends who have supported and encouraged me (humored me) over the years. I hope this little jaunt through my youth and growing up in Coronado will bring smiles to your faces.

It's harsh, looking back, to realize some of us survived while others did not. But I'm here to tell it as I remember it, whether it makes you laugh, cry or cringe.

Don't be too hard on me about exact dates and spellings, and forgive my tendency to celebrate the "sex, drugs & rock 'n' roll" years, but that's just what much of it was, a celebration, an extended Summer of Love.

***

My fascination for the Enchanted Isle after more than half a century hasn't dimmed. If anything, my love and intrigue for what was, is more.

People ask me all the time about what's left from that earlier Coronado—the Coronado of the 1960s and '70s. That's a good question; however, it's not one I eagerly launch into an answer to.

I'd like to say it's the friends I've made along the way, and continue to cherish in my daily life. I like the way the wind creeps over Point Loma at 11 a.m. every morning. It's like clockwork, and still fascinates me. The sunsets continue to be epic and strike deep at my soul. Unfortunately, even more so because of the fires that burn inland as a result of Santa Ana winds every fall. Likewise, the rare appearance of the shipwreck Monte Carlo, after half a dozen brutal storms wash away the sand, is something that has real value to me (the sandbars from this usually bring good waves that time of year, for which I'm also grateful).

I continue to gravitate to the beach to hear the sound of the ocean breaking on the shore. The August swells no longer come in August, but surf continues to feed our cravings at both ends of the island throughout the year. Clayton's remains a memorable breakfast destination, as does the Night & Day Café, known to most of us back then as, "the Greasy Spoon."

When reflecting on what's still here from those old days, one can't help but regret what's not.

One of my biggest regrets is that the car-carrying ferryboats are gone. The train no longer runs the length of the island. Little markets like Free Bros and Lambs are long gone, as are the local eateries Papa Tom's and Oscar's Drive-In.

Even the family restaurants, which were once world-class, have dropped their standards, shortened their portions and raised their prices. Customer service? A thing of the past. And they are so noisy for the most part that conversation is nearly impossible.

Gone are Krishna Mulvaney's, the Chart House and the original Brigantine. Gone is the Chowder House. La Avenida has disappeared, and somewhere in restaurant heaven you'll find Bula's and the original Mexican Village.

All of these thoughts come to mind as I celebrate Heaven on Earth in Coronado and put pen to paper to tell these stories of my youth. Sure, Coronado's changed a heap since I came here in the mid-'60s, but if I squint my eyes, I can still see my Paradise, still see my home this past half century and more, still see the faces and hear the voices of old friends then and now.

Frank Zappa sang, "It can't happen here . . ."

Well, it did happen here.

I'm delighted to be able to entertain you with these memories. And, I'm grateful for that endless stimuli of standing full frontal to the Pacific Ocean for years and years, and of being able to say, I'm still here, you bastards.

You flatter me with the title of "historian," but I prefer to think of myself as a storyteller, passionately in love with Coronado. It's a wonderful feeling to know something you wrote made someone laugh, or cry. If somewhere in this book you find pleasure in my writing, then that will make me very, very happy.

Lord, forgive me the sharpness of tongue, the emails sent without thought, and please don't let my self-deprecation appear as an endorsement for my behavior. It was a different time, the '60s and '70s. I'm grateful to have lived through it all, and this book is in memory of those who did not make it out the other side.

—Joe Ditler, Coronado, CA

CHAPTER ONE

Continuation School: Out of Sight, Out of Mind (1968)

*You know you got to go through hell
'fore you get to Heaven.*

—Steve Miller

That picture in the Post Office wasn't me. I swear. But it could've been, might've been, had I not escaped from San Bernardino. I am the proverbial caterpillar-turned-butterfly on a surfboard.

Find me if you can. One minute I'm sitting in my room somewhere in the Inland Empire listening to the Beach Boys on the turntable. The next, I'm trying to figure out how to apply Paraffin wax to a 10' 2" surfboard along Coronado Beach.

I never learned how to swim (and still can only side stroke a few yards). When taking my SCUBA class, and later my instructor class, I cheated in the pool. I waited until it was near dark and "swam" in the shallow end, where I could walk while making swim motions with my arms.

Fitting in wasn't always my strongest suit. I was bullied since the fourth grade from physical weaknesses stemming from rheumatic fever. I still remember the quack doc telling me, "You physically exert yourself, your heart will stop." Once the word got out that little Joey Ditler couldn't fight back, I was a target for every sonofabitch who wanted to practice his right cross, or gut punch.

One thing I decided when I moved to Coronado was that no more would I tolerate bullies. After a couple of fights, the word got out that the new kid had a quick fuse, a nasty right hook, and didn't fight fair.

It's a long way from Muscoy to the Pacific Ocean. Some called it a ghetto, but it was Muscoy dust I shook off my boots on that first ferryboat ride to Coronado in 1966; when I began to get to know Coronado on weekends.

Muscoy sprawled at the edge of the desert and the foot of the mountains—a tiny piece of middle-class countryside on the outskirts of San Bernardino.

Cajon Pass ran through it, and trains would derail about once a year when their brakes heated up coming down the Pass, sending hobos flying and rolling in the prairie-like landscape. The hauntingly lonely sounds of train whistles and coyotes lulled me to sleep nightly.

Orange groves once fed the economy, but the smudge pots designed to keep the frost away polluted the sky and backed up in the San Bernardino basin. It was so severe that thick brown smog was killing trees at the 3,000-foot level in the nearby mountains.

That was Muscoy: dirt sidewalks, smog, little-engines-that-could, slowly hauling their loads up the Pass day and night. The original headquarters for the Hells Angels was located at the top of my street. At night, barking dogs and wind squealing through poorly fitted windows were a constant companion.

This was home to me. Whitewashed trees lined our little street. Old covered-wagon wheels marked the driveway entrances. I even rode my horse to elementary school on occasion.

My dad called it, "Hell's Half Acre." It was home to three Ditlers, two horses, cows, sheep and goats, dogs, pigeons, turtles and snakes.

Once, just as I sat down on the toilet, a giant lizard swam up through the bowl and made a terrible commotion as he snapped his jaws in the direction of my junk. To this day I lift the lid and take a good, long look before I sit.

That first generation of Hell's Angels used to roar up and down my street on their stripped-down hogs. My German shepherd, Sergeant, would bite at their legs and boots as they rode by. It wasn't long before someone painted a swastika on the street in front of our house. Yeah, I get it now—ignorance; Ditler vs. Hitler. This was the early 1950s, post-WWII years.

People couldn't figure out whether I was greasy/sleazy or darkly cool.

Moving from Muscoy to Coronado in 1967 at 15, I stood out like a lost tourist from the Valley. People couldn't figure out whether I was greasy/sleazy or darkly cool. For a while there they called me a "narc," and that title was hard to shake my first couple of years. That was short for narcotics officer. If you didn't know someone, you suspected them as working for the Man.

I hate to admit it, but drugs went a long way in helping me find my place in Coronado. Leisure drugs, like pot, hash, uppers, downers and even LSD and mushrooms. It goes without saying we all drank a lot of alcohol.

I wore laced, black Beatle boots, Levi bell-bottoms frayed at the bottom, navy peacoat (in all weather), and I didn't wash my hair.

I had extremely curly hair, which was definitely not cool in high school. When it rained or misted, I would become the frizz monster. So, I put Butch Wax in my hair in an attempt to straighten it.

The only way I can describe Butch Wax is as surfboard resin just before it sets up—thick and gooey, and then rock-hard.

The instructions were specific: "Apply the wax liberally to your hair. Take a brush and comb your hair all the way forward into a point. Wait 15 minutes, and then comb it to the rear into another point. Do these steps six times and your hair will be straight."

Well, it did get straight, sort of—what was left of it after ripping it out at the roots in that little exercise. But, when finished, I looked like I was wearing a Kraut helmet. A dirty, greasy Kraut helmet. If someone touched it, they immediately recoiled with a gasp.

Not being the most eager or gifted generation, we struggled through Coronado High School. There were the jocks—the beer-drinking athletes striving to earn their letterman sweaters (and impress the girls). And there were the druggies and surfers. All the druggies cared about was pushing the boundaries of getting high. All the surfers cared about was riding the perfect wave.

At my 25th high school reunion, I was amazed to see the druggies (the ones who didn't die along the way) had cleaned up. For the most part they had turned into successful and creative people—pillars of the community.

Many of the former athletes, on the other hand, sported ponytails and facial hair, and were, well, were what I'd describe as leeches on society. Somehow life in Coronado had gone full circle without my noticing until that night.

During my junior year at Coronado High School, I decided to grow my hair long. It was a time of "mind-expanding" drugs, so most of us were experimenting with LSD and mushrooms and smoking about anything we could roll in a Zig-Zag paper or stuff in a pipe. I sketched the Zig-Zag man on everything I owned—my Pee Chee folders, my text books, my surfboard, my arm, the walls of the restroom.

I ditched classes whenever possible and smoked cigarettes in the park across the street. My grades plummeted and teachers began to warn the principal, Mr. Oliver, that I was a troublemaker. I look back now and realize I was cursed with attention deficit disorder in the extreme. I don't suppose anyone could diagnose such things in those years. Of course, today, everyone blames it on ADD.

Once I was called into Principal Oliver's office. Two teachers and two young school psychiatrists had me do a written test. For once I participated. The test was actually fun. Turns out it was an IQ test. When they called me in to discuss the results, one of the psychiatrists screamed at me out of frustration, "What's your problem? Your IQ is higher than anyone on campus, including the people in this room. Why can't you get good grades? Why don't you even try?"

Teacher, coach and mentor, Robbin Adair.

I just shrugged.

A few days later, an entourage consisting of Mr. Oliver, his vice principal, Mr. Nelson, and the campus truant officer, Chauncy, marched into Mr. Adair's English class with instructions to pack up my stuff. It appeared that my time had come. I was being sent to Continuation School.

Mr. Adair, sweet man that he was, argued and refused to let me go. Eventually, he lost the argument. In hindsight, I'm so sorry I didn't go to his class much. When I did, I sat in back and didn't pay attention. I didn't even know his name at that point.

Yet, this classy man, this dedicated and humane teacher, ordered the men to wait in the hallway as he went to get something for me. As a parting gift, he grabbed four worn, rabbit-eared and extremely used paperbacks and handed them to me.

"CORONADO'S CONTINUATION · OPPORTUNITY HIGH SCHOOL" That is the name of the new school that opened last week in the Glorietta Housing Auditorium. Members of the staff are (l. to r. — Maurice Shaw, principal-teacher, Mrs. Sally Hargreaves and Joseph Cavanaugh. Two concepts underline the new school. (a) The opportunity School is primarily for those students who have had academic, attendance or citizenship problems and need more individual attention and instruction. (b) The Continuation School is primarily for those students placed there by the Board of Education action, generally because of arrests for serious violations of law (narcotics, etc.) Drug offenders will be in separate classes according to Principal Shaw.

Maury Shaw, Sally Hargreaves and Joe Cavanaugh – one tough and determined group of teachers. Grateful to them all.

"You may not appreciate this now, Joe, but some day you will," he said.

The books were J.R.R. Tolkien's *The Hobbit*, and the trilogy *Lord of the Rings*. I did read them, several times over.*

Now you get the picture. Except for a precious few instructors and coaches at CHS (Ron Clark, Pike Meade, Robbin Adair, Coach Satterlee and Coach Nixon), it was a stiff and unforgiving learning institution not prepared or willing to deal with this coming generation or anyone who didn't fit. I surely was one of those.

Coronado was a Navy town in the strictest definition of the term. But the Hippies in Haight Ashbury 500 miles to the north had thrown a stone in the pond, and the ripples from that splash were flooding over little Coronado, influencing the lifestyle, the clothing, the popular slang and, prevalent above all else, the music.

---

*High school English teacher Robbin Adair had given me those four worn and highly used paperbacks in 1968. I wasn't a reader, but I read them, and read them two or three times. Years later I married and had two children, Chelsea and Jack. In 2001, I took my kids to San Diego to see "The Fellowship of the Ring." To my surprise, I saw Robbin Adair walking out of the earlier screening. I grabbed the kids and ran up to him. He remembered me, and we shook hands. "Mr. Adair," I said. "Do you remember those four books you gave me?" He paused, trying to recall. I reminded him, and then told him how they inspired me, and how I read them to my children at night when they went to bed. And how, now, here we were, watching the first Hobbit movie, and how fitting it was that we should run into him. Clearly, in my mind, we had come full circle, and all because of the kindness he showed that outcast hippie kid in his English class in 1968. We both hugged and cried. We remained close friends and tennis partners until he died.

Most of my friends were from Navy families. My own father worked on the Navy Base. Several of these families had husbands and fathers in Vietnam or, worse, in a POW camp. Many had received that knock on the door saying their father had died in action.

I remember a "Twilight Zone" episode from that era, when people were bad, really bad, little Billy Mumy would whisk them away to the cornfield. At Coronado High School in the '60s, you smoked or dealt drugs? They got rid of you. With the wave of his hand, Principal Oliver would whisk you away to Coronado's cornfield, the Continuation School.

Got caught stealing? Off to Continuation School. Missed too many classes or caught smoking cigarettes in the park? Whisk. Threatened a teacher? Whisk.

In my case, the official reason for my banishment to Continuation School was growing my hair too long and refusing to cut it. Whisk.

Although there was strong suspicion that I was anything but an angel at the time, there I was, in the middle of that cornfield, with a pretty wild bunch of Breakfast Clubbers.

Continuation School was located on a grassy area just south of the Municipal Pool, next to the boat ramp along Glorietta Bay. The Naval Amphibious Base bordered us to the south.

Three WWII Quonset huts served as classrooms. Three teachers (whom I suspect were also "whisked") valiantly tried to keep us in line. But, in reality, we were out of sight, out of mind, and it was a pretty loose definition of a school.

Large Torrey pines filled the park. High up in the trees were enormous speakers (apparently from multi-use events held there). At breaks between classes, and at lunchtime, the principal, Mr. Shaw, would allow us to tune in KPRI FM on the speakers and play our music. It was not lost on us that we were hearing the greatest rock 'n' roll in the history of man, as it was being made. Today they call it, "First Generation Classic Rock."

KPRI was an underground station. In the late '60s they would play seemingly forever without commercials, and we would cling to every note. Block parties of Moody Blues, Doors, Country Joe and the Fish ("Section 43"), Buffalo Springfield, Hendrix, Cream—long versions of songs straight from the LP vinyl at the station.

"They'll never build that bridge . . ."

The entire time this was all going on, we could see this bridge taking shape off in the distance. It seemed to grow from each side of the bay until, in 1969, it connected, marking the end of one era and the beginning of another in Coronado.

"They'll never build that bridge," we would say to each other, but today the Coronado Bay Bridge is a factor of life here on the island. It led to carpooling Barrio gangs at first, then more tourism, and now you can hardly drive or park on Coronado in the summer months due to the congestion. The sleepy little Coronado of our youth is gone forever.

Within just the first few years of the bridge opening, we had night-time beach curfews, and development of the Coronado Shores and the Coronado Cays. The train had gone away, the ferryboats had been sold, and the only thing that grew faster than tourism was crime.

* * *

Our teachers at Continuation School were Miss Hargreaves and Mr. Cavanagh. She taught English and history, he taught science and health, and Mr. Shaw filled in where needed.

A chain-link fence wrapped around a tiny dirt space about 8x15 feet bordering the parking lot behind the Iron Walrus—an old wooden pottery shack.

One day I got an idea. I convinced Mr. Cavanaugh to allow students to plant a garden of catnip in that dirt space as a science project. He was delighted at our enthusiasm.

The town was in a marijuana drought at the time. But Dave Adams and Scott Hartland discovered a new source deep in Mexico. My friend Skip Aston's sister Stephanie was Dave's girlfriend, so I was often in their company. One day, Dave walked me out to his garage, which was filled with Michoacán—a very good pot at the time. He asked me to move it for him among my friends.

. . . plastic sandwich bags with five fingers of pot in them.

I suppose at the time I thought it a great way to permanently eliminate that nasty nickname of "narc" I had

Catnip, that innocent little plant that, for about a month, fooled everyone at Continuation School, everyone, that is, except the students.

been given the year before, and make a little cash in the process.

They would give me plastic sandwich bags with five fingers of pot in them. I'd pinch off a finger and sell the rest for $20, half of which went to Adams and Hartland.

In cleaning the bags, I amassed a huge jar of seeds. At Continuation School that week, I laid out my plan. It wasn't hard to recruit fellow gardeners. We dug neat little furrows the length of the lot, planted seeds, then marked every three feet or so with catnip seed packets attached to Popsicle sticks and stuck in the ground.

Students took turns watering the infant plantings. It was a group science project. Mister Cavanaugh would look proudly from his window as we tendered our garden and our little crop begin to grow full and green. We were the dregs of society, and I'm sure it was a feel-good moment for Cavanaugh as he watched us actually working together on a project, any project.

Future lieutenants in the Coronado Company, the international drug smuggling ring that began in little Coronado, were part of my gardening team. Among those who participated either in the planting, grooming or intended sales of the product, included Eddie Otero, Bob Lahodny, John Setter, Al Sweeney and the Acree brothers. I think I sold bags of pot to most of them. I sold the Acree brothers their first pot. I didn't like them, so I cut their product in half and doubled the price just to make them go away. They ended up being directly responsible for the rise (and fall) of the Coronado Company.

About a month later we all arrived at school to find the entire Coronado Police Department (all three units and the Cream Creeper) waiting for us. The science project was roped off and policemen were digging up our huge, extremely bushy plants.

They informed poor Mr. Cavanagh that what we had actually grown was marijuana. Well, it looked like catnip, at least for the first few weeks. Good old Mr. Cavanaugh never ratted out a soul, God bless him, and he gave me a passing grade in his class.

Our punishment, as I recall, was to lose our breaks between class and not be able to listen to KPRI for two weeks. Such was life at Coronado Continuation School.

***

On Fridays. Mr. Shaw made everyone devote the afternoon to a friendly game of softball. Mark Brown decided that was a perfect opportunity to ditch. When everyone went to play ball, he and I took off toward the parking lot.

Funny thing about Mark Brown. He was from a well-to-do and loving family, had everything he ever wanted, but he was a kleptomaniac. He couldn't walk past a four- or eight-track tape deck without stealing it.

As he was trying to unhinge a tape deck from under the dashboard of a VW bug in the parking lot, big Stan Antrim (who ran the municipal pool) reached through the sunroof and grabbed him by the hair.

Mark and I had dropped acid before darting off the premises. The plan was to be well on the road to freedom before it hit us. As we were dragged back to the school by the hair (and we had considerable ponytails at the time), the entire student body stood watching, wondering what would happen next.

It wasn't much of a reunion, just the two of us. But Scotty Burton and I relived a childhood full of memories this day exploring our old haunts along the water at what was once the Coronado Continuation School.

When someone dropped, we all knew who it was, what they had taken, and how much. We even knew where they got it. At the time, Orange Sunshine was the rage. We were all eating it. Indeed, it was a close-knit bunch of little thieves and troublemakers we had down there.

Antrim turned us in to Mr. Shaw, who ordered Mark and me to drop our pants—underwear, too—and bend over his desk. Good old Maurice Shaw. He weighed around 300 pounds, stood about 6' 4" and had a heart of gold. But when he swung that wooden paddle, he thought he was Babe Ruth going for the center-field fence.

I can't begin to describe how awful that punishment was. Not the pain so much; not even the embarrassment; but all the tiny cartoon characters that were leaping out of my eyes and screaming as they flew across the room when that big paddle came in contact with my bare ass. It was almost too much to handle.

Years later I became friends with Maurice Shaw. We were in Rotary together and became very close. I think he was proud that I not only got through those difficult years, but actually made something of myself. And I'm sure he went to his grave believing that swat was what corrected the course of my destiny.

***

There were a lot of people stuffed into those rusting Quonset huts. Some eventually got out. Some went back to CHS. Some dropped out altogether.

. . . *a pretty good wake-up call.*

I was in for quite a shock when June came. I was held back a year. Despite the humbling fact that I had been held back, it was actually a pretty good wake-up call. I petitioned the school that I shouldn't be there because I hadn't committed any crime. They agreed, but the humility of not graduating with my 1969 class hovered over me like a dark cloud. The school wouldn't allow me to be in the yearbook, and I wasn't allowed to attend the senior prom.

The next fall I was one of the Coronado Opportunity School's first students. Opportunity School was a line of small classrooms behind the old police station and near the high school (the corner of Sixth Street and D Avenue). This new environment was more traditional classroom-looking, and we were treated more like students than outcast rebels. At lunch, music again became part of our daily ritual. I brought in an old portable turntable. Every day at lunch I'd play Cream, Hendrix, Traffic and Buffalo Springfield.

Because we could work at our own speed, I worked fast. With the help of night classes and long days, I successfully completed my senior year, again, and was out of high school in two months. Eventually I got degrees in journalism, English and photography at Southwestern College and San Diego State University. For some of us lucky ones, life goes on, it seems. Bumpy road? Yes. But, in hindsight, I was the first person on either side of my family to achieve a college degree.

***

Years later, in 2016, I ran into old friend and Continuation School alum, Scotty Burton. I hadn't seen him since 1970, but we had recently connected through Facebook. He was visiting Coronado for a few days, and we had lots to catch up on, ranging from first girlfriends and Mrs. Long's garage, to who tapped for us on Friday nights (adults willing to buy minors alcohol, no questions asked).

We talked of those taps, old Mickey and Gobbler O'Brien; we reminisced about drinking Ripple and Red Mountain wine at North Beach around a fire ring, and whether we got to third base with certain girls.

We remembered what teachers we hated and the ones who were kind to us. After all, we were just a couple of kids with ADD before its time. And we were both of such a sense of humor that we didn't mind poking fun at how foolish we were back then.

The first thing Scotty wanted to do was to get a three-egg special at the Greasy Spoon (memories). We did. Then I made him get on a bicycle, and we rode down to our old alma mater.

The park is still there. The Quonset huts long gone. The Iron Walrus is still standing, but no sign of "catnip" crops. The Torrey pines are gone, and that bridge in the distance? It looks like it's here to stay.

CHAPTER TWO

Party at Alonzo's House (1968)

Fact: Coronado sold more alcohol per capita in the 1960s than any other city in the United States. In the 1950s, we were voted the safest place to raise children. God knows nobody was prepared for what the 1970s would bring.

My first home in Coronado was the Reid Hotel, an enormous brownstone that was the tallest building on the block. It was at the corner of Orange and B Avenues, where Bank of America now sits.

My dad had a small room on the second floor, and we crammed in there for a year. Later, we rented a small place near the Hansen Mansion on A Avenue, and then my parents purchased a run-down, one-bedroom home at 424 B Avenue.

This is the story of 424 B.

Many will remember that address as the site of an infamous party on November 10, 1968. It wasn't my house when the party took place, despite what Coronado Police officer Bob Paseman (ret.) tells everyone these days at a local bar. I wasn't even at the party, although I attended plenty of others around town.

Coronado in the late 1960s and throughout the 1970s was the scene of hundreds of beer-keg gatherings, cheap wine beach bashes, skinny

Crowd Jams Little House, Then Jail Cells

20 Police Sent To Noisy Affair, Seize Marijuana

EVENING TRIBUNE Dispatch

CORONADO — One hundred and fifty persons, 39 of them juveniles, were arrested at a party in a one-bedroom house here last night, when police found marijuana at the party.

The party-goers were held in connection with narcotics offenses and with disturbing the peace.

Lt. Jack Rose said numerous complaints had been received about the noise at the party and, after repeated warnings, 18 officers were sent to the house at 424 B Ave., to break up the party.

Small Quantities Found

Rose said marijuana was found in the house in small quantities.

Four youths, who apparently organized the party, Rose said, were also held in connection with violation of a business and professions code which forbids the sale of alcohol to minors.

Rose said the gathering was a keg party in which a person pays a dollar to get in and is [...] to drink beer.

None Got Away

The officers surrounded the house at 11:30 p.m., Rose said, and then knocked on the door. None of the party-goers escaped the raid, Rose said.

Several of them got up in the attic trying to hide and fell through the plaster ceiling," Rose said. "What a mess that house is."

"It's incredible that all those people could get in that one little house."

4 Cells Packed

Rose said all four cells of the jail were packed with the party-goers. He said it will take all day to process the arrest reports.

"We are still trying to establish exactly who the person or persons are who rented the house," Rose said. "With 150 persons to question, we are

(Cont. on Page A-4, Col. 2)

150 Arrested in Raid

CONTINUED FROM PAGE 1

having trouble getting clear answers."

Rose said there was no music at the party, not even a record player or radio.

"They were just packed into that house like sardines, drinking beer," he said.

No Resistance Offered

Rose said that except for the people who went up into the attic, none of the party-goers offered any resistance. He said most of those arrested were transferred to county jail today.

About one-fourth of those arrested were girls.

One of the persons who left the party shortly before the police arrived said the house was being rented by three students at Southwestern Junior College.

Were Being Evicted

He said the three were being evicted this week because of previous parties.

"They had these parties every weekend," he said. "Since they were being kicked out of the place, this was the last fling."

EVENING TRIBUNE

PHONE 234-7111   4 PARTS — 48 PAGES   SAN DIEGO, CALIF., MONDAY, NOVEMBER 11, 1968   10 CENTS PER COPY

150 Arrested in Raid On Coronado Party

The headline that rocked an island.

dipping at Gator Beach, bike races and naked pool parties. No one was exempt.

We didn't have a grapevine or coconut telegraph, but when someone's parents were out of town for the weekend, word traveled rapidly. "Keg party at the Sweeney house."

The Sweeney/Johnson house was just one of many gathering places. In this case, it was made up of two families, merged through marriage. There were 13 kids total, ten of whom were living in the house at this time. Down the street, in the McLeod family home, there were eight kids. We were all very close. That's the way Coronado was.

The Sweeneys, like the McLeods, had a fair-sized swimming pool in their backyard. We didn't have Pandora or iPods or iTunes. What we had was one underground FM radio station around the far end of the dial. Yup, you guessed it: KPRI provided the soundtrack of our young lives for many years.

An evening at the Sweeney or McLeod house usually began with a few beers, a joint and a few girlfriends. It didn't take long before it was utter chaos. As the night went on, there might be 100 or so people crammed into the house, loitering in the yards or naked in the pool.

We were on the heels of the free-love generation, where sex, drugs and rock 'n' roll prevailed. And, if needed, there was a Free Clinic in Imperial

Officer Bob Paseman, a royal pain as a rookie, but loyal friend later in life.

Beach so the family doctor (Dr. Dill) couldn't lecture us, or rat us out to our parents when we picked up something funny.

On that warm November evening of 1968, 424 B most certainly danced its most unforgettable dance. It was, it turned out, the final hurrah for the little party house/crash pad that had been giving police and neighbors fits for months.

While living there in subsequent years, I heard many first-hand accounts of how people either got away or went to jail that night, or what they went through to avoid capture. I only wish I had written them all down at the time.

As the story goes, when the cops arrived, Lee and Judy (anonymity requested) squeezed into the attic crawl space only to fall through the thin ceiling; Carol and John were making love in a beaten-down Eugenia bush alongside the driveway; Tommy "The Laz" put a lampshade on his head and crouched in the corner, figuring the cops would mistake him for a lamp. The house reeked of marijuana smoke, stale beer and sex.

All that party house needed was a family and some TLC. Here is 424 B Avenue after we had moved in. My German Shepherd Frauline was perhaps the greatest dog a man ever had. The house stood and was our home until demolished in 1989.

Police cars surrounded the place on streets and in alleys. Large prisoner buses were parked a few blocks back. A shrieking, ear-piercing whistle went off and the Coronado Police Department crashed through the front doors while simultaneously converging on alley access and over neighboring fences.

Kids were handcuffed and dragged to the station by the dozens. The *San Diego Evening Tribune* reported 150 or more were arrested; mostly minors—many of those being young girls.

All night long, parents (comprising the greatest number of retired admirals and admirals' wives anywhere on earth) screamed and banged on the police desk to "Release my kid!"

Big Jim Darnell, Coronado's deputy mayor, showed up with bail for his son in the form of quarters from his laundromat, $615 worth, to be exact. To make a statement, he splattered all 2,460 quarters on the counter and walked out with his boy.

Is it any wonder things like Outlaw Bike Races and the Coronado Company grew from this soil?

This was the night little Coronado was shaken as never before or since. The memories of this night, although often embellished over the years, are still spoken of with a wink and a snicker by those over the age of 60. Is it any wonder things like Outlaw Bike Races and the Coronado Company grew from this soil?

Alonzo Smith, Dean Atkinson, George York and David Lindsey had rented the house. They had been handed eviction papers and decided a final party was just what was needed. They put up posters at Southwestern Jr. College advertising the party.

The night of the big bust was actually the fourth night in a row, with each party growing larger, culminating with the night of November 10.

"At $2 a head, we collected a little over $300 by nine p.m.," Dean Atkinson told me years later. "The cops showed up about eleven-thirty. They basically came in the front door. They had the gate by the garage [on the alley] blocked off. People started to scramble everywhere."

Sandy McLeod recalled there were three McLeod siblings at that party. "Yes. Me, my older brother and younger sister. My brother was eighteen so he got hauled to county jail. My mom came and got my sister and me out pretty quickly."

At little Coronado Police Department, dozens of rowdy kids were screaming and yelling for their parents. One, Bobby Mathewson, ripped a pay phone from the wall and threw it at the police. "I swear, I just leaned on it," he would say years later.

Gary Carter sneaked out of the house that night and, while walking past the police station, saw a large bus. As he walked around the bus, he saw his friend Gary Maltby looking out the window and screaming for Carter to call his mother.

"He threw me a piece of paper out the window with his phone number on it," said Carter. "Then others started to yell their phone numbers at me. People were throwing wadded up notes out the window with their phone numbers.

"I made my way to a pay phone across from the wrestling room at the high school," said Carter. "I only had a quarter, so I called Mrs. Maltby and one other, and then went back to the bus. I told them I didn't have any more money, and I couldn't make calls from home or my parents would wake up. People started throwing dimes, nickels and quarters from the back of the bus at me."

Rex Gammon had had his share of adventures with the Coronado police. They had left him with finely honed instincts when it came to impromptu getaways. When they barged the house, he quickly scaled a wooden trellis to the neighbor's roof. "In one leap I had hold of the roof and a bathroom vent pipe and pulled myself up. Once on top, all I could see were police cars," said Gammon.

"They were in the front, the alley, at the end of the block. There must have been twenty or thirty of them. The police and Alcohol Beverage Control agents were yelling and grabbing everyone, and people were trying to run anywhere, only to be stopped at every possible exit.

"I crouched down and started running across the roof to the opposite side," said Gammon. "I thought I could jump to the next house. The houses were close together on that block, maybe a ten-foot leap. I ran as fast as I could. I cleared the span but the next roof was wet, and I slid down to the overhang and then to the ground."

Rex crawled under an old tarp and lay perfectly still for hours, until everyone had gone. He was one of the lucky ones and lived to brag

I'd give everything I own to have them back, my dog and my dad.

about it that night at the Greasy Spoon. Keep in mind, this was little pre-bridge Coronado, where the entire town was usually lights out and in bed by 8 or 9 p.m., except for the police and occupants of the Greasy Spoon.

Inside the tiny CPD jail cells, kids were crammed and stacked every which way. "I was there, too," said John Little. "I saw the police putting up perimeters and thought I could run through them. But, I had one too many beers and my vision and legs were not fully functional, so I decided to stay in the house. The police kept escorting us out a few at a time. I was one of the last to be arrested."

John Little, the class clown, is an immensely successful attorney today, but hasn't lost his sense of humor. "I was thrown in a jail cell and did entertain the crowd with some of my best material, but soon felt queasy and had to lie down on the concrete floor. I found a small space under one of the bunks.

"...the whole place and everyone in it began to spin."

"It was not a big cell and there were double-digit people crowded in it. I tried to sleep, but when I closed my eyes the whole place and everyone in it began to spin. I lost my dinner, and since I was lying on a slight incline, much of it drained down on to me. Not the way I had envisioned the night ending."

In the end, all the arrests were thrown out on technicalities, and the worst damage was a night or two in jail. The Coronado Police took the hardest hit. It was years before they had a working relationship with the community.

* * *

The infamous party at 424 B is history now.

It's sad what the party-goers did to that little house that night. The cottage was barely standing afterward. But the owners patched it up, and it went on the market the next month. My folks picked it up for $26,000. We lived there happily from 1969-1986, when my wife Eva and I took it over.

It was a little 1922 beach cottage—single-wall construction, added-on sun room, trunk room, garden shed and garage. Asbestos shingles coated the exterior and even the smallest of earthquakes could make this rustic bungalow do the Mambo.

My family kept the home until 1989, when we sold my parents' $26,000 investment for $400,000 and moved to 1034 Encino Row. To show you how property value soared in tiny Coronado, we bought the Encino Row house for $399,500, lived there until 2018, at which time we sold it for $2.3 million.

The 424 B house was bulldozed and the lot split. The new owners constructed a pair of John Gillem-designed-and-built "Long Tall Narrows" that quickly sold. I doubt the current residents at 424 B have any idea of the ghosts that haunt that piece of dirt. Only the pepper trees in front remain as witness to that explosive night and my colorful youth.

Somehow most of us got through the 1960s and subsequent '70s. The party scene, like the bike races, faded into history. It's amusing how even the most horrific of events and memories can seem so hilarious all these years later.

And those pepper trees? Well, sometimes I find myself walking or riding my bike past them and I stop. I walk up to them, place my hands on their coarse and rippled trunks, and say a few words from the heart. Funny how that just feels like the right thing to do. We survivors, after all, have to stick together.

CHAPTER THREE

KPRI, Underground Radio (1968)

There goes the last DJ. Who plays what he wants to play.
And says what he wants to say, hey hey hey.
And there goes your freedom of choice.
There goes the last human voice.
There goes the last DJ . . .

—Tom Petty

In the '60s we had no clue. I remember hearing President Bill Clinton being interviewed about smoking pot. His response? "I smoked a little pot as a teenager, but I never inhaled."

I think my problem was, I never exhaled.

My room was small. It was originally designed as a slant-roofed trunk room, on the rear of the old, falling-down party house at 424 B. Yet, I was pleased. It was private. It was my own space.

A four-pane window opened out to a yard and large pepper tree. My German shepherd would stand on her hind legs and keep an eye on me through the window, climbing in when darkness fell to sleep with me and in general protect me. My neighbor to the south was Joey Simpson.

The home of KPRI-FM, the underground rock station, located at 7th and Ash, downtown San Diego. KPRI photos courtesy Nick Schram.

To the north was Johnny Falletta. Neither seemed to mind the smell of marijuana smoke emanating from my room.

Once in a while I would take out all the furniture, except for cushions and pillows on the floor and against the walls. My friends and I would gather back there as our refuge from authority.

An eye hook in the ceiling dangled a long string with a roach clip at the end. We would affix a large joint to it, light it, take a big hit and set the clip swinging in a wide arc at about chest-level. As we lay back on the pillows, blowing smoke rings at the ceiling, someone would reach out to grab it, then the process would start all over again. Or, if it went on long enough, we would just sit there and stare at this mildly entertaining act.

When we were finished, we opened the door and an explosion of smoke preceded our exit. One by one we left the room and walked through the kitchen to the front door. "Good-bye, Mrs. Ditler. Nice to see you," they would mutter as they walked past my mother—shirts and pants dotted with roach burns and droppings from the swinging roach clip, some of them still smoldering.

The KPRI mixing board, source of great magic and mixing of music over the years.

It was the soundtrack
of our young and carefree lives.

All the while, the music of KPRI filled the air. It was our backdrop. It was the soundtrack of our young and carefree lives. Sometimes I think back in amazement at what I put my parents through—long hair, one-night stands, loud rock 'n' roll, mind-bending drugs. I can tell you that, during this period, I never went to sleep without my FM radio on low, KPRI dialed in, and a smile on my face. The dial light would be the only illumination in the room until the sun came up.

***

KPRI 106.5 had been around most of the 1960s. The DJs played a lot of Dean Martin and Frank Sinatra. Then, in December 1967, the concept of keeping the station on the air after their customary midnight sign-off time was tossed around.

The idea was the brain child of young Navy man Steve Brown. He

The cast and crew of KPRI-FM at the 1972 Reunion. In the front is Preacher Man. Middle row, from left, OB Jetty, Solomon Grundy, Bün T. Phens ("Uncle Ben"), Inor Gaddim, Ceci (KPRI fan), Jim Twogood (fan). The photo bomber in rear is Jim LaFawn.

came to KPRI right off the street and pitched his idea to station manager Larry Shushan. Steve volunteered to do those three hours a night for no compensation. His only caveat was that he could play any kind of music he wanted, and what he wanted to play was raw, uncut rock 'n' roll like we'd never heard before (or since).

He hit the airwaves with the radio handle of "O.B. Jetty." Suddenly, during the night, when Dean Martin and Frank Sinatra were sleeping it off, the music of Big Brother and the Holding Co, Grateful Dead, the Doors, Animals, Moody Blues and a variety of San Francisco sounds, were bouncing around the airwaves of San Diego.

It didn't take long for listeners to discover this new show. Word travelled fast along Coast Highway and inland. He called these late-night jaunts, "musical journeys into the unknown," and his unique brand of music was labeled, "Electric Music for the Mind and Body."

From left, OB Jetty, Nurk, Inor Gaddim and Uncle Ben, seen through the glass window so many of us stared into late at night, in an effort to be part of what was clearly rock 'n' roll history in the making.

Soon other eccentric radio disc jockeys joined him with names such as Acmad the Revolving, Inor Gaddim, Captain Sunshine, Gabriel Wisdom, Solomon Grundy, Preacher, Publius, and of course, Bün T. Phens ("Uncle Ben").

Similar experiments were taking place in San Francisco (KMPX/ KSAN) and Los Angeles (KPPC). All three stations received high listenership, with low-key, heavy rock format. This new breed of radio station had no hype and very little advertising. The commentary was as important as the music, as the DJs bantered back and forth with serious knowledge of the music they played and the musicians playing them. Were they progressive rock stations, underground rock stations, outlaw rock stations, or all of the above? Whatever you wanted to call them, we loved every minute of it.

Vietnam had its Adrian Cronauer. Mexico and the LA Basin had Wolfman Jack. San Diego had O.B. Jetty, Inor Gaddim and Uncle Ben.

Within six months KPRI changed their format to 24-hours of musical journeys into the unknown, "All rock, all the time!" became their slogan. Soon KPRI was all anyone talked about. *Billboard Magazine* did a major article on the station, and that gave it huge recognition—the cachet it had been looking for. KPRI became a household word.

The station had gained a reputation as being an underground rock 'n' roll phenomenon. Throughout this time period, KPRI sponsored hundreds of concerts, from the Beatles, Janis Joplin and Rolling Stones, to Country Joe and the Fish, Lee Michaels and Moby Grape. Their popular concert series included every major rock 'n' roll act of the time.

While attending Continuation School in 1968 and '69 as one of a couple of dozen outcasts from society, I sat on the rocks along the bayside of our park area and listened to KPRI between classes and at lunch. FM radio was new to us, and especially this sort of station.

One day we listened to a DJ called Gabriel Wisdom (now a respected La Jolla financial adviser) as he interviewed LSD guru Timothy Leary. The latter was stoned out of his gourd and fresh out of jail; the former was just a teenager, a college student, but seemed to zone in pretty damned well with Leary.

In 1969, actor Dennis Hopper visited the station. Ron Middag, aka Inor Gadim (Middag spelled backwards), recalled that night. "I did the interview. He came to the station with a woman from some ad agency to talk about an upcoming movie none of us had heard of called, 'Easy Rider.'

"He was wearing the same fringe leather jacket and leather hat he wore in the film. I think I was the only one in the studio who had ever heard of him. I remembered him from the film "Rebel Without a Cause," even though his hair had grown long and shaggy since that film.

"After the interview he asked if there was a back door. It was clear he didn't want to continue his tour of San Diego radio stations. We jumped in my Triumph convertible and made our getaway. I just happened to have a big bomber in my pocket that we toked up and it was off to the beach."

The DJ and the actor drove around all day long, touring local beaches and listening to KPRI's music on the radio. Hopper crashed at Middag's place that night, a sort of commune on Mt. Helix where he lived with nine roommates.

"My roomies were used to me coming home with the odd hippie or long-hair," said Middag. "No one seemed to recognize Dennis Hopper, and I think he enjoyed the anonymity of the evening. We had a large meal and he crashed on the couch. The next morning, I drove him to the airport."

Such was a day in the life of a KPRI DJ.

Years later, KPRI-FM was immortalized in Cameron Crowe's movie, "Almost Famous." Crowe hung out at KPRI as a kid. The studio was recreated entirely for the film.

In 1968, the British band, The Who, came to San Diego to support its new single, "Magic Bus." They stayed at the El Cortez Hotel, and after the show the band walked across the street to KPRI studios to hang out with this American underground radio station they had been hearing about.

"I was there that night," said Uncle Ben. "They came to see one of our DJs, Greg Willis. Pete, Keith and John from The Who stayed until six a.m., requesting records and answering our dorky questions. They were wonderful fun to be with. Keith Moon was so funny. Greg let him DJ for a while that night, which really lit up the phone lines."

KPRI was the only station I heard during that decade to play long versions of songs from the '60s. They would play the seven-minute version of The Doors' "Light My Fire," a nearly nine-minute version of Creedence Clearwater Revival's "Susie Q," the eleven-minute version of the Chambers Brothers' "Time Has Come Today," and even the twenty-two-minute version of Arlo Guthrie's "Alice's Restaurant."

As Uncle Ben recalled fifty years later, "Other DJs envied our freedom on KPRI."

There it was, our favorite song, but stretched out to something akin to a live jam. The long versions lingered across the country in smoke-filled rooms and broadcast from low-wattage radio stations. Everything prior to this was two minutes, twenty-nine seconds, as dictated by the FCC and radio stations of the mid-1960s.

The Rolling Stones' "Goin' Home" was eleven minutes long. As Keith Richards said in his biography, "Making an LP usually consisted of having two or three single hits and their B-sides, and then filler." To create more filler, they would just extend their hit songs.

When The Doors released "Light My Fire," it was a little more than seven minutes. Many of the Top 40 radio stations tried to do their own edits, often butchering the song. Finally, Electra Records put out an official single edit of the song at just under three minutes. But, long versions were there to stay. That sort of musical filler often came in the form of a hit song not originally intended to be so long, but drawn out from two and a half minutes to nine minutes (Buffalo Springfield's "Bluebird"), seventeen minutes (Iron Butterfly's "In-A-Gadda-Da-Vida"), and, in the case of Jethro Tull's "Thick as A Brick," 45 minutes—an entire album side.

We never knew when one was going to be played on the radio, but many of us clung to our FM radios, set to the outlaw stations, the renegade stations, the stations that weren't afraid to buck the rules, and KPRI in San Diego was the best of those stations.

In researching supplementary facts for this book (and my memories), I located and interviewed another of those notorious and original KPRI DJs, Uncle Ben. His real name is Nick Schram. My first question was about the long versions. I wanted to know what prompted them to play which one, and why.

"It depended on a lot of things," he said from his home in San Francisco. "Long versions gave DJs freedom to take a long dump, smoke a joint, or get down with our girlfriends on the back couch."

Later he admitted it wasn't unusual for a cute girl, smiling at them through the window from outside, to be invited inside the studio.

He locked himself in the studio and played the Beatles' "Hey Jude" for four and a half hours.

I remember we often took the old, car-carrying ferryboats across to the mainland, had lunch at People's Fish, shopped at Ferrer's Surplus, and then walked up to the KPRI studios at Seventh and Ash.

We would look through tinted and curtained windows to watch the DJs do their thing. Sometimes they would invite us in and talk to us, or get stoned. Sometimes the curtains were closed, and now we know why.

One October day, however, Uncle Ben went rogue. He locked himself in the studio and played the Beatles' "Hey Jude" for four and a half hours.

I remember listening in the car as I checked the surf at sunset, but had to go in for dinner. I unhinged the radio from under the dash and ran into the house, grabbed a plate of food, locked myself in my room and turned on the radio. I sat there mesmerized at what was going down for the entire event.

Of course, I didn't have a real FM house radio in those days. I had the radio from the station wagon. I'd bring it in, hook it up to my Lionel model train transformer, and turn the power dial until the radio lit up and began to play. If I had too much power, it would overheat. It was a MacGyver sort of improvisation my dad hooked me up with, but it worked. The train set went away with my youthful innocence years prior, but that transformer was like gold.

Uncle Ben's typical attire in those days was a top hat and flowing cape. It was 1968, and he had apparently been experimenting with mind-expanding drugs, too. He got it in his head that he wanted to play "Hey Jude." Well, he played "Hey Jude" alright, for four and a half hours.

Long versions were one thing, but playing the same song for most of your shift was pushing it, even for KPRI.

As one song ended, the second turntable started up mid-song with another "Hey Jude." If the record started to skip, Uncle Ben would slap the needle arm out of the way, creating the all-too familiar squeal of a 45-rpm car crash. Then I would hear the vinyl record explode into the wall or window, as I recall.

Someone would bang on the door for him to let them in, first with kindness and a gentle, condescending voice, and then with violent pounding and the threat of his job. Nothing phased Uncle Ben.

Ron Middag was program director at KPRI at the time (he now continues to sling hard-core rock 'n' roll from Buzz 107.5 on the island of Maui). He remembered clearly the night "Hey Jude" took over the airwaves.

"Steve Brown had been deployed to Vietnam, so I was the program director at the time," said Middag. "I was at home when I heard "Hey Jude" repeating itself. I got in my car and drove down to the station as fast as I could.

"I remember thinking, 'What has he done now? He's really gone off the deep end.' When I arrived, it was chaos. There were people gathered on the corner of Seventh and Ash and the station phones were ringing off the hook.

"My thoughts and fears were changed the moment I got there. When I walked in, I saw that he had really tapped into something. 'Hey Jude' was at that point our most requested record at KPRI. What Ben was doing was really creating a lot of energy.

"I didn't try to stop him, but I did answer some of the phone calls. Most of the callers were women, and most of them were crying. The men were screaming, and people were just worked up in general. None of us had ever heard of anything like this before.

"I was able to route the studio feed through the production room so I could take the calls saying little-to-nothing, and feeding their comments under the music, which only added to the chaos.

"At one point the police arrived and I had to talk them down," said Middag. "They had received calls saying that someone had barricaded himself in the studio and they wanted to know if there were any hostages involved. I assured them that was not the case and they went away."

All this while, Uncle Ben continued to party on with his listeners.

"Waaaaaaa waaaaaa waaaaaaaaaa," he would whine on the air. "I'm blowing my mind. You can't come in here. I'll never stop. Follow the bouncing waaaaa waaaaaaaa waaaaaaa."

Meanwhile, to his thousands of listeners, "Hey Jude" continued to march on hour after hour as hypnotized young listeners such as myself sat glued to the radio, staring at the 106.5-FM dial light, afraid to miss a single outburst, not knowing what the hell was going on but caught up nonetheless in the hysteria of the moment. At that point, it was hard to tell who was more stoned, the DJ or the listeners calling in.

Records continued to skip and get thrown against the wall. A record would meet its end. No problem. He played another. And another, and another. Uncle Ben was a man on a mission.

One lady called in on the air and said, "I'll pay you fifteen dollars if you play it forever." Another woman called and said, "You're beautiful." Still another said, "God loves you." Someone called in and said, "Far out, man." Then a caller in a straight voice said, "Would you play 'Hey Jude' by the Beatles?"

To this day, I cringe when I hear that song, but I tell you honestly that Uncle Ben's "Hey Jude" party ranks right up there as one of the great and seminal events of 1968.

More recently, while interviewing Uncle Ben about this, his only response to that evening was, "I guess I got caught up in the moment. I remember when I put on my top hat and cape to leave, there must have been a hundred people outside the building waiting. I ran like a madman to my convertible, did some circles in the middle of the street while honking my horn, and everyone was certain I had lost my mind."

At a reunion of KPRI DJs held recently in San Diego, Uncle Ben summarized his "Hey Jude" marathon simply: "People cried . . . the police came."

He now refers to me as, "Coronado's biggest KPRI fan." I accept that honor. I sometimes catch myself daydreaming of my dark bedroom, with only the dial light illuminating a small patch of the room, and never knowing what song was next or how it would be introduced.

In those days, we grew to anticipate such in-studio tricks as wide stereo separation, feedback and vocal distortion. It all sounds so primitive to describe today, but to us it was a revelation. One night I sat with make-shift speakers on either side of my head, grooving on Jimi Hendrix's guitar and wah-wah pedal swinging from one speaker to the other in radical sound separation, from one side of my brain to the other.

This was the fresh and raw soundtrack of our lives, a musical wallpaper like no other, introduced by DJs with odd names who became etched in our memories.

It was a celebration of that great musical frontier, that first wave of rock 'n' roll that has become so revered over the decades. The kind of rock we only find commercial-free on Sirius XM, iTunes or streaming. Long live First-Generation Classic Rock.

Long Versions of Songs From the '60s/'70s

1. Harlem Nocturne (1960), by The Viscounts [8:11]
2. Light My Fire (1966), by The Doors [7:08]
3. Time Has Come Today (1966), by The Chambers Brothers [11:03]
4. Susie Q (1968), by Creedence Clearwater Revival [8:37]
5. In-A-Gadda-Da-Vida (1968), by Iron Butterfly [17:3]
6. Alice's Restaurant (1968), by Arlo Guthrie [22:31]
7. Machine Gun (1969), by Jimi Hendrix [13:00]
8. Thick as a Brick (1972), by Jethro Tull [43:54]
9. Bluebird (1973), by Buffalo Springfield [9:06]
10. Passion Play (1973), by Jethro Tull [45:00]

CHAPTER FOUR

Underbelly of the Bridge (1968)

"It'll never happen," we all said in 1968. Then, in 1969, we gave it such names as "Bridge to Asgard" and "the Rainbow Bridge." I still refer to a trip to San Diego as, ". . . crossing the bridge to America."

To this day some people won't drive on it. Others refuse to drive in the outer lanes. One woman I know takes the Silver Strand to family events in San Diego, while her husband and children brave the bridge. She just won't drive on it.

Another woman I know does a pre-flight drill with her kids before they cross the bridge that includes leaving doors unlocked, windows cracked, and specific instructions on what to do should they survive the fall. She tells them things like, "Hang on to your sister's hand the entire time, wait until the car fills with water before opening the doors," and, "Head straight to the surface and stay together."

No kidding.

I still have this recurring dream that I'm driving on the bridge. It begins to separate at the top, and I wake up as I'm leaping to the far side with arms and fingers outstretched. So far, I've always managed to

The underbelly of the bridge, the workers' catwalk. Here it is seen many years after our teenage adventures up there. The floor grating looks much more solid and dependable now. When we walked on the old one, it sagged under our weight. Photo by Dale Frost, courtesy SD Maritime Museum.

wake up before I reached the other side, or didn't. Oftentimes I'm clinging from the far side by my fingertips as the world falls away around me.

Such was the dramatic transition from slow-moving, car-carrying ferryboats to a state highway in the sky.

During construction of the bridge, an access catwalk was built underneath for the workers that soon became our playground at night. It wasn't very wide—maybe three and a half feet. It was constructed of wire mesh so when a person stepped on it, the floor pieces bowed under the weight. Handrails were about waist high and unstable.

Once workers realized my friends and I were climbing out on the catwalk, they built a tall, locked gate on the Coronado side to keep us off. That didn't work, as we just swung under it with as much effort as transiting a set of monkey bars on the school playground.

We'd take our girlfriends on the catwalk after dark. Guaranteed trip to second base! They hung on to us with both hands. They seemed, to a person, to think that their lives depended upon it. Maybe they did.

The night was to us, you see, as Sherwood Forrest was to Robin Hood.

CalTrans built other deterrents, but we always seemed to find a way around them. That's how it started, and always under cover of darkness. The night was to us, you see, as Sherwood Forrest was to Robin Hood. We thought we were safe there.

Photos courtesy Coronado Public Library.

Before the bridge, ferryboats carried people across from San Diego. Photo by Frank Jennings, courtesy Coronado Public Library.

I remember how spooky it looked as I fixed my gaze ahead. The catwalk grew dark and foreboding as it curved out and over the bay. Nobody wanted to go, but no one wanted to admit they were scared. All the stuff I told my kids to never do, we did with reckless abandon.

Girlfriends were usually bold at the start, because we weren't very high up at that point. But then . . . then, it got crazy. We stepped gingerly on each wire-mesh screen. It bent down nearly a foot, which made us grab the rail tighter. If too many grabbed the rail at the same time, well, you can imagine. We would space out, but that was worse for those in back. They felt frighteningly alone once the people in front disappeared into the dark.

Darkness enveloped us quickly. There were no lights on, in or below the bridge. The cold sea air howled through the unprotected catwalk area, freezing the water in our eyes and the spit in our mouths. Sometimes a piece of the flooring was missing. That was tricky, but we managed to get around the holes.

Then, once we were about 180 feet over the water, we came to a door—a large, circular door that resembled a watertight hatch on a ship. We opened it, crawled through, and suddenly we were walking on cement in what appeared to be a large container. The three middle spans are all like that.

According to urban myth, the middle sections were created to float, in case the bridge went down in an earthquake, and the shipping channel had to be cleared with tugboats. At the time the bridge was built, there was a

The ferryboat Crown City, carrying a full load of cars across the bay to San Diego. In the background, the bridge slowly begins to take shape. The coming of the bridge changed little Coronado forever, sadly. Photo courtesy Coronado Public Library.

huge U.S. Navy mothball fleet moored in South Bay. I remember reading once that the mothball fleet was the fourth largest naval flotilla in the world.

I've interviewed the designer of the Coronado Bridge, Robert Mosher, and he denies the bridge was ever built to float. However, I tend to subscribe to the theory they built it with that in mind, then realized how ridiculous it was and changed their story. If not for the water-tight bulkhead hatches at the ends of those three main sections, I might agree with him. Or, maybe the real reason is not embraced by mainstream media today for security purposes.

Of course, the bridge hadn't quite connected in the middle when we began to do our little nighttime treks, so we would go as far as we could, then sit and hang our legs over the ledge and open a beer or light a joint. Girlfriends would slowly begin to breathe again, but would also smother us boys in hugs and kisses out of sheer gratitude for keeping them safe.

**Within the year,
our small town
would be gone forever.**

Below us a much slower city and harbor tucked in for the night. We could see the car-carrying ferryboats slowly making their way across the bay to the northwest of us. Little did we know at the time what a strange and ironic drama was unfolding in our lives, nor did we have any idea how this bridge would change Coronado.

Within the year, our small town would be gone forever. In its place would be a major tourist destination with rapid and unlimited access to the outside world. Was it worth it? No, I don't think so.

With the bridge came escalating property values. Family-owned restaurants and businesses began a trend of falling to the wayside because they could no longer afford rent. Restaurants continue to charge more and give smaller portions. Nowadays, all we really have left of old Coronado is the memories. Most of my friends can no longer afford to live here, and I'm rapidly becoming one of them.

***

I remember the last day the ferryboats operated. The arrangement, due to a non-compete clause, mandated the ferryboats cease operation at midnight August 2, 1969. As the "Ferryboat Finale" read (the historic certificate handed out to passengers that final day), "This certifies that the bearer of this certificate rode the San Diego-Coronado Ferry on its last day of operation, August 2, 1969, climaxing 83 years of service to the San Diego and Coronado communities." It was signed by James C. Haugh, president of the San Diego and Coronado Ferry Co.

The final five car-carrying ferryboats were the Coronado (arriving here in 1929), San Diego (1931), North Island (1939), Silver Strand (1944) and Crown City (1954).

My friends and I wanted to ride that last ferryboat, but waited until the end of the night so we could actually ride "the last one"—the final passage across San Diego Bay.

Cars that had been lined up waiting half way down Orange Avenue, half way across town, slowly began to drive on to the old and creaky wooden decks of the ferryboat. Then, we pedestrians walked aboard. I

In 1998, the Star of India, the oldest merchant sailing ship in the world, sailed for the first time under the Coronado Bridge. I can be seen at the tip of the jibboom, legs in a life and death grip, and frantically shooting photos, thus making me the first person to sail Star under the bridge. Photo by Navy PH1 Cavanaugh.

remember looking up at the name board. We were on the San Diego, it was 11:30 p.m., and we were headed for San Diego. As we pulled into the creosote-soaked pilings, the captain rang his ship's bell and pulled the whistle lanyard for one long, last blow. "Everyone off," he yelled. "End of an era. You've just ridden the last ferryboat."

Well, you can imagine our confusion. We argued with him that we had to go back to Coronado. He couldn't have cared less about us as he grabbed his jacket and lunch pail, and headed toward the off-ramp of the boat.

Three of the girls in our group said they were going to swim home, and one said she would leave her new boots on the dock to retrieve the next day. Years later I discovered they just wanted to get rid of Bob Pickford and me. They walked to a phone booth and called one of the girls' mothers.

I couldn't swim (still can't) and Pickford didn't want to get his hair wet. You had to see his hair to understand. It was a tightly-packed mass of curly chaos. Out of desperation, we began going car-to-car in the long

Museum director, waterfront reporter, and too stupid to realize that if I fell I would probably die. In those days I was fleet of foot and fearless whether going aloft or making time with Euterpe on the bow while underway at sea. Photo by Kenny Andersen.

line of automobiles waiting to catch the last ferry. Those folks, too, it seemed, misread the fine print.

Finally, we found a young couple in an MG convertible. They were awfully giddy, so we figured they had gotten stoned for this auspicious occasion.

"Say, how would you like to be the first to cross the Coronado Bay Bridge?" We were going car to car with that line before we found the stoned couple in the MG.

Once they realized they weren't going to go on the ferry, they began to see the magic of our proposal.

So, in a manner of speaking, we became the first hitchhikers to cross the Coronado Bay Bridge that night. We sat on the convertible top that had been folded over the back seat. Like being in a parade, we drove over that big scary bridge, waving at everyone we saw.

For the next couple of years, we drove the bridge at night, in darkness. Lights weren't installed until sometime later, when Coronado activist Carol Cahill pushed the Coronado City Council to install them.

Prior to that, we would frequently find ourselves driving home from a concert or dance, and we would stop at the top of the bridge and get out of the car.

In those days, as mentioned, Coronado had a habit of going to sleep about 8 p.m. Even though the bridge was open 24/7, in those early days there was virtually no traffic at night.

We would hike a leg over the rail, light a cigarette or joint, and pull the pop-top off a can of beer. We would turn up the radio and KPRI would entertain us with cutting edge rock 'n' roll—Paul Butterfield's harp, Eric Clapton's guitar, harmonies from the Moody Blues, the pounding of the Stones . . .

Sometimes we would pee over the side and watch as it floated down like a giant lasso with darkness as our cover. It was all fun and games for us in those teen years. New was the fact that we could drive. New was the Coronado Bay Bridge. And you know what? We would sit up there partying for half an hour or more, in the dark, and never see another car crossing the bridge from either direction.

The bridge is about 200 feet tall. If you jump and hit the dense salt water from that height, your bones shatter like landing on rocks. That's why few survive a jump from the middle spans. I think at this point there have been 400 jumpers. Most of us, longtime residents of Coronado, have lost friends and loved ones to that fate.

The catwalk is still there, and has been modified for safety over the years. But, unless you're with CalTrans or the Port of San Diego on official business, you won't ever see it.

For us, growing up in Coronado in the 1960s, it was a little slice of Heaven to be able to climb out there, snub our noses at authority, and

feel, for a few fleeting moments, as though we were on top of the world
. . . our world.

***

In a way, the bridge began to define this new era in Coronado. Dare-
devil pilots would fly between the pylons; people would jump—some
with parachutes, most without. The bridge was force fed into our Coronado culture in a way no one could have expected.

I was development and marketing director at the San Diego Maritime Museum from 1989-2002. We would sail the tallship Star of India
periodically, and I campaigned to do something we had never done—
sail the Star under the Coronado Bridge. I reasoned that it would be the
media event of the year. It was.

When Star of India sailed under the Coronado Bridge that first time
in 1998, I talked the skipper, Captain Richard Goben, into letting me
climb out on the jib boom with my cameras.

He had brought all the Star crew back on board, out of the rig and
off the boom, because even he wasn't sure what would happen when
the winds reversed, which they do (as every sailor knows) when passing
under the bridge.

Seasoned crewmembers and old sailors alike cowered beneath the
Star's cabins and rails when we passed under the big blue span. Even
though the Star's mast is only 100 feet, they were freaked out by the il-
lusion of closeness as we sailed through.

. . . trembling in the scuppers as the bridge's shadow enveloped us.

I got a kick out of that. Some of them were really scared—old sword-
fishermen who had survived perfect storms at sea; retired military officers who had lived through Kamikaze attacks in WWII—all trembling
in the scuppers as the bridge's shadow enveloped us.

Meanwhile, I'm sitting on the tip of the boom, legs wrapped tightly around, facing backward, and shooting my cameras with both hands at the cloud-like squares'ls of the Star billowing at me. Crazy stuff!

I used to take great joy in telling people I was the first person to ever sail the Star under the bridge. Being situated so far forward on the jib boom, I was, literally, the first.

Even though the old Star was barely making headway, it all went by extremely fast. We had a tow line from a tug off our bow, just in case. But just before we went under the bridge, the line went slack and the sails filled with wind. I looked up as we passed under the bridge. There, on the catwalk, was my dear friend, Dale Frost, photographer for the Port of San Diego.

The bridge is still here, and, true to predictions, Coronado will never be the same. Today, every trip across the bridge finds me slowing a bit as I approach the top. I put my hand on the head liner and say a prayer to the Lord in gratitude for bringing me to this little island paradise back in 1966, and for allowing me to stay here well into my senior years.

CHAPTER FIVE

Don't Call Me "Cripple" (1968)

Surfing drew me to Coronado back in 1966. My estranged father was living here and I was, as mentioned before, living in Muscoy. One day, at the height of my despair, I received a letter from him. In it was a Greyhound bus ticket to San Diego and a photo of a Carl Ekstrom surfboard—a 10′ 2″ beauty with asymmetrical tail and like new.

The letter was short and sweet: "Joey, I'm sorry I haven't been a better father to you. But I've found work down here in a little place called Coronado. I think you would really like it. I'm hoping you'll come down for a visit, and take a look. Enclosed is a bus ticket and a little something I bought for you. Love Dad."

Needless to say, that next weekend I was on the bus and on my way to Coronado. Of course, it wasn't quite as easy as that. I got on the wrong bus, and it stopped at twelve towns along the way. Then, when I arrived at the bus station, in deep, dark San Diego, surrounded by whore houses, tattoo parlors and Shore Patrol vans, there was no dad. He had forgotten I was coming.

Dad was an alcoholic back then. Scared as I was, I found my way

The two things that brought me to Coronado in 1966 were a Greyhound Bus ticket and this surfboard, a 10'2" Carl Ekstrom with asymmetrical tail – way ahead of its time. I still have it. Photo by Jack Ditler.

to the ferryboats, then to Coronado, then to the Reid Hotel where he lived. He wasn't there either, but the hotel manager drove me to a little Spanish-style house and said, "Your dad is in there. But don't tell him I told you so."

I knocked on the door. A woman answered, and there, in the back room, I could see my father, pulling on his pants. He had been drinking and carousing, and indeed had forgotten I was coming.

. . . *my life was changed forever.*

As you can imagine, he was extremely upset at himself, and after a fashion I went back to his hotel with him. That next morning, I awoke early and walked past Oriental Imports and down Churchill Place to the beach. It was a breathtaking experience for me. I realized at that moment I had found paradise, and my life was changed forever.

With Dad's help, I pulled out the surfboard. It had been a custom board made for young Charlie Free, Jr., son of the local butcher. Charlie was headed into the SEAL Team and had to sell his new board.

I needed help to carry it to the beach. But I figured out how to put wax on it and paddled out to receive my first lesson in respect for the great Pacific.

That went on for a few days, then on every weekend possible I returned, again by bus. By summer, I was here for three months, and then transferred here officially in my junior year of high school.

I never seemed to get better at surfing, but I continued to try. Boards were heavy and I was too skinny. One day, lying on my back on the beach the kids now call "Dead Larry's," a small rain cloud passed overhead. My chest was so concave it collected water. Get the picture? Wimp, pasty-skinned, frizzy-haired inland dude from Berdoo.

It was too heavy to carry by myself, but I usually found someone to help. Seen here on the new surfboard in Imperial Beach, shot from the IB Pier. Let the adventures begin. Photo by Jack Ditler.

One of my first friends was Bobby "Booty" Mathewson. He, too, was disenfranchised with surfing those heavy boards. He had worked a deal with Richard "The Joker" Jolie, down in Imperial Beach, to shape him a kneeboard. Joker's surfboard shapes would become world famous in a very short amount of time, under the banner of South Coast Surfboards.

Well, that sounded cool to me, so I wedged my way into the deal. Soon we had two new kneeboards—his orange, mine blue. I donned a pair of swim fins and began to kneeboard with a passion. I fell in love with it. I could carry it under my arm on my bike, toss it in the back seat of the car, quickly get out into the lineup. I could even duck dive it.

Riding a kneeboard, however, required me to be on the defensive

The only thing that lured us to Mexico more than surf was beer and tequila. We are seen here at the Long Bar with legendary bartender Ramon in the background. From left, Gayle Hakes and Gary Risley, Jill Coons (my girlfriend at the time), me, Lil' Debbie (Don Harris behind her), Mike McCartin and Bart Tucker (rear).

all the time in the lineup. I found myself constantly validating my presence out there, as though I were a second-class participant. I realize now that I was at the bottom of the food chain, just as boogie boarders and "sweepers" (stand up paddlers) are today. Waves these days are, as they were then, territorial. You had to earn your place in the lineup. I realize now that all that splashing with my fins was a horrible distraction that most felt did nothing but draw sharks.

But I was getting waves and getting noticed. I charged on that little board—a single fin, with rope handrails put in by Bob Duryea, who owned our island surf shop, Du-Ray's. Because of my low profile on the wave, I could get stuffed deeper than most—could tuck up into just about any barrel, as long as it wasn't too big, because what I couldn't see I was deathly afraid of. When surfing, my glasses sat on the beach in a towel.

In 1970, I followed some buddies out at Three-M's, near San Miguel,

It must have been too busy to sit at the Long Bar's long bar. Seen on this late-night Mexico adventure are, from left, Richie Heinz and a woman he met at the Hotel Del, Susie Davis and Bill Lyons, Mark Thomas and Jennifer Hakes, her cousin Val and me in my fashionable corduroy jacket. No idea who the big Mexican guy is, but he loved our women and he just wouldn't give up.

in Baja California, Mexico (Three-M's is no more, fallen to construction). I was rapidly getting noticed by The Bros—a group of surfers my age who had nicknames like Slow, Goob, Maestro, Bird, Crab, Mar, Dewey . . .

Surf was twelve to fifteen feet that day, big A-Frames coming out of deep water. I was scared shitless. As a teenager, I was too stupid to know I shouldn't have been out there. Couldn't swim a lick, and I was blind as a bat.

Everyone ripped. Everyone, that is, except me. I would kick my fins to the brink of the wave, then pull back white-faced, deathly afraid to make the drop. It was just a big blur to me. If I couldn't see the bottom, I wouldn't commit. The Bros, for the most part, indulged me in the lineup only because I stayed out of their way, and I got waves. But on this day more than once I heard the chicken call, "Bek bek bek BEEEEEEEK" from guys in the lineup.

Some of them, like Bob DuRay and Jimmy Reilly, were encouraging, even taking time to coach me. Finally, after two hours and a session they would boast of for years, my friends had all gone in. They had logged a perfect session and surfed until exhaustion. I continued to kick my fins and traverse the outer reef looking to find a smaller wave in. No one was in the water but me and little Jimmy Reilly.

Even Little Stevie Wonder could have caught a wave with that kind of help.

JR and I had an arrangement. Being so blind in the water, he graciously allowed me to follow him around in the line-up and benefit from his wave knowledge (and good eyesight), as long as he got the first set wave. It was a beautiful relationship. Then, in theory, the next wave or waves in that set would break in exactly the same position. Even Little Stevie Wonder could have caught a wave with that kind of help.

By then, however, Jimmy was tired and losing patience with me. He paddled over and said, "Look, Ditler. Either take the plunge or sit out here by yourself, but I'm going in, and I'm taking my eyes with me."

After a few minutes by myself, I came to realize the blurry drop couldn't be any worse than being blind and alone in the very active kelp beds of Mexico. Suddenly, I heard imaginary splashes behind me; felt stuff touching my legs underwater. That fear alone drove me to paddle into one of those big Mexican freight trains. As I dropped over the edge, my stomach was in my throat.

Half way down the face I was still on my belly out of sheer fear, board, legs and fins flapping as though I were being dragged behind a truck on the interstate. But I made the drop. Purely by accident my board caught the inside rail, cranked a turn, and flew back up the face. What an epiphany!

It was, quite simply, the most thrilling thing I had ever done at that point in my life. Suddenly, I was working that monster, stuffing myself deep in the pocket as it pitched out and over me toward shore.

I dragged myself up on to my knees and kept carving the face on the inside, hoping that some of the guys were watching. Funny thing about near-sightedness. Nothing beyond your field of vision seems to matter. As I raced toward the beach, I neglected to recognize how close the shoreline was. Blind Owl, that's me.

I hit the shallows with incredible force and was catapulted head-first from my kneeboard onto the beach and into a massive chaos of stinky, spongy-wet darkness.

Stunned, I sat there for a second with my ass sticking up into the air, trying to decide if anything was broken. When I tried to push off, my hands would sink into the muck surrounding me. The smell made me gag. I could hardly breathe.

I finally fought my way out only to realize I had launched my young, blind, stupid, long-haired self into the decomposing belly of a dead elephant seal. It must have been there for weeks.

Upon that sudden realization, I also noticed there were carnivorous maggots everywhere—tens of thousands of them, and most of them were on me.

I must have burst its stomach upon impact, because there was this incredible stench that engulfed me in a death grip. I had maggots crawling in my hair, which, back then, was thick, curly, and down the middle of my back. The maggots got into my ears, my nose, my mouth. I began to vomit in every direction.

I ripped off my wetsuit beaver tail and threw it in the water. Then I followed it in, desperate to get rid of the maggots and the smell. Nothing worked. My hair was rife with them. I must have really pissed them off, because they just wouldn't let go. They were crawling all over my body. I could almost hear them yelling collectively, "Fresh meat, boys."

By the time I made it back to the campsite, everyone had eaten breakfast, finished lunch, and the food was all gone. As I hobbled up to the fire, Alec MacKenzie yelled, "How was it, Cripple?"—an unpopular term of endearment for anyone who didn't stand up on their board.

My friends wouldn't let me ride in their cars because I smelled so bad. Finally, Mike McCartin said if I gave him gas money, I could ride on the back of his Honda-305 motorcycle. I did, clinging to my kneeboard all the way home to Coronado. The border guards were tempted to run us through secondary, but changed their mind once they got a whiff of me.

The indignity of suffering molestation by a dead elephant seal was bad enough (the maggots by then were dried and caked into my wind-swept snarls of hair). But calling me "Cripple" because I didn't stand up on the wave was a blow to my soul that I couldn't ignore.

Within two weeks I had invested in contact lenses, and I bought a lighter longboard. I've been standing ever since. Eventually, over the years, I even dragged out the old Carl Ekstrom on occasion, and learned to work that special surfboard and piece of family history—my key to Coronado in 1968.

I've been blessed
to have made it out of Muscoy . . .

To this day, every so often, I have this dream that I'm being attacked by maggots on a lonely Mexican beach, but I still wake to the sound of crashing surf in Coronado. I've ridden a lot of boards since then—short boards, twin fins, thrusters, eggs, Outlet sleds, but eventually came back to the longer boards. Now I ride a 10'6" Encinitas Surfboards single fin.

When the wind turns offshore, the tide is on the ebb and a swell is running, I grab my longboard and head down to take a look. I've been blessed to have made it out of Muscoy to become what I'd always dreamed of becoming—a surfer.

I may not be the best surfer in the lineup day in and day out, but I hold my own, big or small, and no one calls me "Cripple" any more.

As a postscript to that story, my mother wrote to my father and me from Muscoy, where she had remained when I made my pilgrimage to Coronado. She asked if she could visit us. After being here for only a couple of days, she too declared it to be her "paradise." She and my fa-ther got back together and our family ended happily ever after.

In many ways, Coronado has been the glue, the magic elixir, the formula for happiness in my family both then and now.

CHAPTER SIX

Newport '69 &
End of World Concert:
The Forgotten Pop Festivals
(1969)

Forgotten pop festivals? Indeed. And it seems I had forgotten about them, too. Then, recently, in an old box, I found a ticket stub. On the back I had scribbled, "Mike McCartin and I were here." It was dated June 20, 1969. I put on some tunes and, like an awakened amnesiac, the memories flooded back.

Before Woodstock, before Altamont. In the days when Jimi's wah-wah pedal could stop a train, and Tina Turner's dancing could shake a bird from a tree, 200,000 of us jammed into the former racetrack, Devonshire Downs, hungry for the rock 'n' roll experience of a lifetime.

Newport '69, they say, paved the way for Woodstock and motivated the Hells Angels' takeover at Altamont. All I know is, I was there, and, after lots of reflection, it seems I even remember some of it.

Mike and I had been kicked out of Coronado High School because we wouldn't cut our hair. We were just shy of 18 and drifting somewhere between the afterglow of Haight Ashbury and the fear of Vietnam.

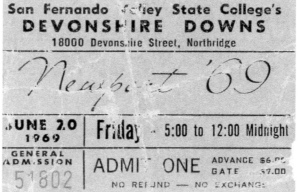

Ticket stubs I somehow managed to save from Newport '69 and the Palm Springs Pop Festival. Not that different from Woodstock, but receiving far less publicity. If Woodstock had taken place in Southern California, it would have had a different legend. The billboard outside the drive-in movie theatre playing host for the latter read, "Tuesday Only, Palm Springs Pot Festival. From 6 to Midnight. Come High and Stay High."

Our lives were unwittingly influenced by our environment - long hair, earthy girlfriends, rebellion, free love, tie-dyed shirts, VW busses, mind expanding assessments, and all to the pounding background of the greatest rock 'n' roll ever.

We heard about this pop festival in San Fernando. It would later be known as Newport '69. We rigged curtains in my '61 Ford station wagon, packed our sleeping bags and some canned goods, and headed north.

What a car that was. Long and low, three-in-the-tree (slang for a three-speed column shift), tail fins and a sporty two-door look. An FM radio under the dash boomed music through two enormous, homemade speakers on the rear floor of the wagon. We tuned into underground stations—the original KPRI in San Diego (of course), and KPPC in Pasadena. If the signal wasn't clear, I had an eight-track tape player in the glove compartment. Gas was 35 cents a gallon.

That first day, Friday, we found parking on a grassy hill just outside the concert area. We parked at the top and walked down to the concert. The hill was abandoned except for us.

Our tickets got us in, but there was no instruction manual to walk us through what came next.

They didn't talk much.
Just smiled, did the slow-motion
bobble head thing and passed the pipe.

A typical scene in those days. The difference being the weed was weaker than it is today, so things like "Bogarting that joint" were common. You took a hit and held it in as long as possible. Quantity versus quality. Photo by Al Sweeney.

Typical of good pop festivals, there was the stage—the heart central to everything else. But, like an artichoke, you had to peel away layer after layer of thorny to unveil the soft and tasty heart of our little rock 'n' roll society.

Immediately off the stage were the mellow folk—drifting about in an eternal cloud of pot and hashish. They didn't talk much. Just smiled, did the slow-motion bobble head thing and passed the pipe.

Mike McCartin and I were besties in those days. His mom turned me on to tuna fish for the first time. Mike and I went everywhere together, including the pop festival, Newport '69. Here I'm trying to get to first base with Debbie Packard (still trying!), while Mike's girlfriend snaps a photo. Note the abalone ashtray beside me. Photo by Jennifer Jordan.

The psychedelic layer came next—people flying high on acid and mushrooms. They smiled, too, but it was a circus smile of a thousand smiles, constantly reacting to out-of-body flights, uncertainty, fear and self-doubt, the sudden all-knowing, and then (hopefully) a soft landing.

Beyond them were the pill freaks and drinkers. They were hard as nails. Don't fuck with them. They were sluggish in speech and action, but quick to anger. They usually ended up crashed in a variety of positions that resembled wrecked cars in a junkyard. Then, on the outer perimeter, were the guards, the outhouses, minimal food access, and constant movement and chaos.

Once the initial shock wore off, Mike and I wiggled our way through the layers of 1969 society and the clouds of smoke to get close to the stage. That was our home for most of those three days—within ten feet of the very platform our vinyl heroes were springing to life on.

The music was out of this world! Tiny visual and sound bites still exist in my memory: Lee Michael's drummer Frosty, tossing his drumsticks in the air mid-solo, and playing bare handed until they bled; CCR; Taj; the hypnotic Cocker; Tull's flute; Burdon; "Time Has Come Today" . . .

The actual list of performers was incredible: Ike and Tina Turner, Albert King, Edwin Hawkins Singers, the Jimi Hendrix Experience, Joe Cocker, Southwind, Spirit, Taj Mahal—and that was just the first day.

On Saturday, the entertainment included Albert Collins, Brenton Wood, Buffy Saint Marie, Charity, Creedence Clearwater Revival, Eric Burdon and War, Friends of Distinction, Jethro Tull, Lee Michaels and Frosty, Arthur Lee and Love, Steppenwolf and Sweetwater.

On Sunday it was Booker T & the MGs, the Chambers Brothers, the Flock, the Grass Roots, Johnny Winter, Marvin Gaye, Eric Burdon and Mother Earth, Poco, the Byrds, the Rascals and Three Dog Night.

Concert promoters were disappointed at Jimi Hendrix's performance

There she is, in all her green glory. The 1961 Ford Ranch Wagon. Two-door. Three-in-the-tree shifting. My chariot for most of our adventures in those days.

Friday and talked him into coming back Sunday. Jimi more than made up for it with an incredible Buddy Miles jam that can still be seen on YouTube.

Half way through the first night, fences collapsed under pressure of those ticketless souls driven by the music to get closer any way they could. Someone had the stupid idea of putting a local motorcycle gang in charge of security. Their badges were club colors on the back of sleeveless Levi jackets. Their tools were baseball bats employed to enforce their point.

For us peace/love Coronado boys, it was a shock beyond words to see those guys cracking the skulls of people crawling under hedges or over fences. They walked around high on power like *Lord of the Flies*, eager to inflict their law without remorse or consequence. The blood flew. It was a nightmare, so we stayed close to the stage and tried not to look behind us.

Even in those days it was not uncommon to spot someone you knew at a concert or festival. Sure enough, Frank Vido came waddling through the crowd, making a beeline toward us.

"Boys," he said in his best gangster voice. "Got some acid for ya. Free. But it got wet coming across the border, so just stick your finger in and grab a lick."

Seems it was a wooden wine keg with a false bottom. In that hidden area Frank had a couple of hundred tabs of Orange Sunshine, the LSD rage at the time.

The barrel got crunched and wine seeped in, dissolving all that acid. No telling how much acid we were licking off our fingers, and, of course, Frank encouraged us to "take more, take more."

A couple of hours later, another Coronado familiar face stumbled into our laps. Dennis Thoms. He, like Frank, was even more derelict than us. They were high school friends of ours, but, in truth, they traveled in a different sort of group, one that was fond of barbiturates, downers and as much acid as they could shove in their mouths.

Dennis was pretty far gone. He could barely speak. He put his head in Mike's lap and passed out. Suddenly, we realized he wasn't breathing. Mike put his head on the grass and we took his pulse. Nothing.

Rain began to fall about this time, and when everyone tried to move all at once we got scared. We had no idea what to do about Dennis's dead body. So we ran with everyone else seeking refuge from the storm.

Somehow, we made it to my Ford wagon. The concert area and the pretty grassy hill had turned into a mud bath of unbelievable proportions. All along the hillside were hundreds of tents, sleeping bags, VW busses, but no people. Thankfully, the concert still held them captive.

"NOW DIT-LAH!"

My Ford wagon wouldn't start so we pushed it down the grassy slope. Picture this: Me driving in reverse, popping the clutch every ten seconds; Mike pushing on the front, screaming "NOW DIT-LAH!" and then leaping on the hood, hanging on for dear life while I back-ended my way down the dark night, unseeing in the rain, swerving in the mud, going faster and faster.

We ran over empty tents and sleeping bags, through makeshift concession stands, and finally at the very bottom of the hill, the old gal's tires caught on the hard road surface and she started up.

We hit the freeway and looked in the rearview mirror most of the way home. As we tried desperately to ignore the acid flooding through our minds, rain continued to pelt the windshield. I found I couldn't see through the rain drops because of my condition.

Anyone else wouldn't have had a problem with that, but all I could see was the slow-motion splatter on the glass, the endless wiper blade movement, the next crop of rain drops, seemingly larger than the last, exploding in my foreground, distracting me from anything beyond that windshield.

At first, we slowed to 25 mph, then had to pull over on the shoulder and wait it out. We never really felt safe until we were on the Coronado ferryboat.

Of course, I'm leaving out lots of the story. But, some things are better left to the imagination. All I know fer sure is, love me some rock 'n' roll, and that was a great time to grow up in Coronado and witness culture-changing music up close and firsthand.

Now I think I'll put that ticket stub back in the box, and the memories with it.

Oh, and I should probably mention that, a week later, Dennis Thoms waltzed up to Mike and me at the Orange Julius, asking why we left him there in the rain. It was all we could do to laugh and hug that dumb sonofabitch. He was alive, and we felt a heck of a lot better about ourselves.

***

"The End of the World Blues Festival"

A few months earlier a similar experience had taken place. As I write this, it's been half a century since these events happened. None of us had any idea 1969 would be so eventful in our lives, much less that some country boy from Muscoy would remember it sufficiently enough to write about it 50 years later.

If there was one underlying theme in the closing moments of the '60s, it was our music. Notice how I refer to it as "our" music. Indeed, it was, and still is. But, also wafting around the rafters, like a slowly dissolving smoke ring, was that transition from drugs to meditation and spiritual awareness. Some made the jump, some would eventually; some died, and others just kept wafting around in those rafters.

In our time "the end" had been predicted by Edgar Cayce, Jeane Dixon, Jim Jones and even Charlie Manson, just to name a few. If enough people predict it, eventually someone's gonna be right. Cayce followers narrowed down his prediction to April 1969. And that's where I come into the picture.

The year 1969 needs no clarification; no explanation. If you don't know our state of mind that year, you haven't been paying attention. Or, as some would have you believe, if you remember the '60s, you weren't really there.

In April, I joined a mass migration of hitchhikers headed to Palm Springs from all directions, for what was being unofficially billed as "The End of the World Blues Festival."

It took three rides hitchhiking before I arrived at twilight with four dollars in the only good pocket of my torn Levis. The scene was three miles east of Palm Springs, in Cathedral City—a place called the Sunair Drive-In Theatre. For the foreseeable future it became home, and the Palm Springs Pop Festival, despite what the marquee broadcasted:

"Tuesday Only, Palm Springs Pot Festival. From 6 to Midnight. Come High and Stay High."

The lineup of musicians blew me away—the Steve Miller Band, Ike and Tina Turner, Eric Burdon and the Animals, Buddy Miles, Savoy Brown, Canned Heat, Moby Grape, Procol Harum, Blue Cheer, the Flying Burrito Brothers, the Jeff Beck Group (with Rod Stewart) and the Paul Butterfield Blues Band. John Mayall performed, and Lee Michaels was there with Frosty on drums.

The day of the concert more than 5,000 people filled the drive-in. Organizers tried to lock the gates, but those on the outside began to get creative. Some broke holes in the fences and pushed their way through. One man was shot and killed by police.

This was my situation: No tickets, darkness falling, music starting, police everywhere, shirtless longhairs freaking out on bad acid (me included), and I'm wondering, "WTF?"

I spotted a couple of longhair dudes crawling through a hole in the fence just behind an equipment truck. "I can do that," I thought.

Someone yelled, "Halt or I'll shoot," and I froze. There was this little fat rent-a-cop waving a flashlight at me. Before I could respond, the spotlight across the way turned from skyward to directly at me. When it hit my eyes, I went blind. Times like that, for fear of the Man, you just tell yourself, "Drag your ass through the hole, dummy."

The smoke lay heavy like a pungent English fog in a low budget movie. John Mayall was playing on stage; Johnny Almond was blowing his horn.

Just a few yards ahead sat a group of people. All I could see was their silhouettes backdropped by the stage lights, and the odd pipe bowl being lit, but I kept crawling toward them as a voice behind me shouted out, "Ohhhh nooooo you don't." The little fat cop had followed me through the hole in the fence.

Before I could turn, the entire audience yelled back at him, "Ohhhh-hhhh yes he does." Within seconds I was being dragged into the middle of a mass of bikers and hippies. They were hugging me and passing the peace pipe. Years later I would liken it to Pee Wee Herman in the biker bar.

Eric Burdon performed the long version of "Sky Pilot." Ike and Tina sang "Proud Mary." Paul Butterfield played "The Work Song." Canned Heat sang "Going Up the Country." If nothing else, we were ready for the end to come, and baby, we were goin' first class.

"I was stoned for a month last night."

The last thing I remember is being on my back and looking at millions of stars above. The night was cold and smoke was still awfully thick, but my new biker/hippie friends created a wonderfully warm circle around me. I felt safe. I felt lucky. I didn't know a soul, but I was grateful for their love.

A guy in a top hat and sporting a long goatee shook my shoulder and passed me his pipe. I'll never forget his shirt. It said, "I was stoned for a month last night." The back of his jacket said, "Hells Angels, San Bernardino." My people, ha ha ha.

When I awoke it was morning and the desert sun was baking the ground. People had scattered; trash was everywhere; but two sisters with dark, waist-length, braided hair, long dresses and headbands were sitting nearby, giggling at me.

They said the party had moved to Tahquitz Falls; that I should follow them. But first, they wanted to get breakfast. We walked through a residential neighborhood, where they stole a bottle of milk from someone's front porch.

At the Falls, people were lounging around in various stages of undress. It was really a sight. I'm sure I was no less a sight, with my long, scraggly, blonde hair and dirty clothes. So, the three of us dropped it all and dove into the pool.

Clean and refreshed, we began walking along the foot of the cliffs, back toward town, when this bearded fellow with a pompadour strolled up to us. It was Wolfman Jack!

He stopped just short of me, cocked his head to the right, then to the left. I did the same. He smiled and said something I didn't understand, then handed me a bag that said, "Wolfman Jack's End of the World Instructions." The bag was as empty as the threat of the great quake. He walked away, smiling and chuckling in that wheezing black voice of his.

Wolfman Jack was my hero. Many a late night I had lain awake under the covers in Muscoy, listening to him on XERB, on my AM transistor radio.

He would howl like his namesake, and then sing along, or offer counsel to young black girls calling in for love advice. For years his audience thought he was black. The Wolfman was King of the airwaves.

The world didn't end that day, but I had the adventure of a lifetime for a 17-year-old kid, and listened to some of the greatest music of my era.

A couple of days later I had hitched my way back to Coronado with phone numbers of the two hippie sisters written on a folded milk bottle top. They were French Canadian, and we would hook up many years later, again in Palm Springs.

In the end, music saved the world, and the Hells Angels saved me.

The Wolfman is everywhere, man. Rock out baby,
we gonna do it right here. Rock 'n' Roll yourself to death.
Have mercy baby, give us some more.
Awoooooooooo . . .

—Wolfman Jack

CHAPTER SEVEN

Hitchhiking Through The '70s (1970)

It was a different time. We logged more miles with our thumbs than anything else. Had to get somewhere? Stand on the curb and put our thumbs in the air.

Since the Great Depression, hitchhiking had become the preferred mode of transportation for the masses. Hobos rode trains. The rest of us hitched rides.

Over the years and decades, the art of hitchhiking continued to develop and become accepted into the nomenclature and societal norm of transportation worldwide.

The art of hitchhiking is simple. We position ourselves on a busy thoroughfare, face the oncoming traffic, and put our right thumbs in the air, pointing the direction we're headed.

A quick assessment of your mobile audience dictates whether you hide your hair in a ponytail or let your freak flag fly. After the first dozen cars pass us by, and desperation settles in, little tricks begin to seep into our routine. Perhaps we try to look tougher; perhaps we want the innocent look, so as to appeal to families driving by.

Whatever we do, we never want to show fear; always hitchhike with confidence. Eye contact is important, because if we do get picked up by a weirdo, that's where the first clue will be—in his eyes.

Maybe we inject a little motion in our wrists or elbows to enhance our dire circumstance. Claudette Colbert, in the hit 1934 film, "It Happened One Night," hoists her skirt, revealing a sexy leg. No thumb necessary for her. She got a ride and caught Clark Gable as well.

"Where ya headed?"

Whatever the technique, there is always that moment when someone slows down to pick us up. We run to the passenger side, and then deal with our fears before opening the door and placing ourselves at the mercy of this complete stranger.

As we lean in the window, we and the driver assess the situation simultaneously. Usually the driver says, "Where ya headed?" At that point we're just so damned relieved to be off our feet and moving in a car that our fears disappear and we focus once more on our destination.

Throughout the '60s and '70s I used hitchhiking as a major form of transportation—the getting from point A to point B. Hitching to

Clark Gable and Claudette Colbert in "It Happened One Night." Their hitchhiking scene remains the ultimate lesson on how to get a ride. Photo courtesy of Columbia Pictures.

Tom Moran and I had the hitchhiking experience of a lifetime trying to get home from Northern California one night. This is a rare shot of him flying his freak flag. Tommy was one of the finest surfers of his day, and was a hippie for only a short period, but, oh my, what a time we had.

Southwestern College—then called Southwestern Junior College—however, was a challenge to even the best of us.

I really had to get one ride down the Silver Strand and to the end of Imperial Beach, at the bare minimum. Hopefully, the ride could get me as far as L Street in Chula Vista.

From there it was a straight shot out to Otay Mesa and that new junior college we all seemed destined to attend, again and again and again over the years, like a bad episode of "The Twilight Zone," or the movie "Groundhog Day."

Long hair, wire-rimmed glasses and all the markings of Mister Cool. Truth be known, we had turned the corner. Transcendental Meditation was our new high when this photo was taken. Photo by Jim Robeson.

Then, at times, I would get picked up by another student and taken to the door of my first period classroom.

Coming home was a looser event, as I had no time constraints such as attendance call in first period. In fact, if I got stuck in IB, I could hang at the beach, visit the Free Clinic, or chow down on a machaca burrito at Jalisco's before trying my thumb once again on the Silver Strand.

There were no pressures coming home. Every detour and every delay, proved to be just another adventure waiting 'round the bend.

I made some wonderful friends along that route during those years. I met some future girlfriends as well. In fact, once I met a cute girl in a '68 VW convertible—metallic blue. She was trying to sell it.

We really clicked, good chemistry from the first smile. She took me to dinner and then to her place. I don't know if that was intended to get me to buy her car, but I was so impressed with her, and her car, I borrowed the money from my dad the next day and bought it.

That retired my thumb for a couple of years, until I discovered the VW was rusted out on the bottom from a previous life in the Midwest, where they salted the winter roads.

Mike McCartin and I on our beach cruisers, checking the Arizona girls hanging out at Center Beach. I had a favorite rock just to the left of the stairs. I called it the "three o'clock rock." I spent endless hours there as a kid, people watching, tanning, making clouds disappear. Then, the City built a bathroom next to it. Life was never the same.

I sold it to Igor Vido. He claimed it was the best car he ever owned and drove it for a long time. Maybe I was premature in diagnosing death from rust.

Once, however, hitchhiking to Southwestern, I was picked up on the Silver Strand by four men in a Chevy Monza. Small car, barely able to house four full-sized men, but they stopped and asked where I was going.

I said, "Southwestern Junior College." They motioned to get in.

I was directed to the middle seat in the rear, between two of the men. They looked like young sailors as far as I could tell—stocky, with muscular builds, butch haircuts.

But I was soon to find out they were red-neck boys who didn't like long-haired hippies. At the time, I had long blonde hair well below my shoulders.

They missed the turn off for 5 North and instead headed south to the Mexican border.

I quickly asked to make a U-turn and head back up the 5 toward L Street. They ignored me. Not a word was spoken the entire time I was in their car.

Finally, faced with the fear they had plans to do something really awful to me, I explained that the Mexican border guards were sure to stop their car when they saw my long hair.

Maybe they would, maybe they wouldn't, but I know that had happened to my friends and me recently, while traveling south to party at the Long Bar.

"And they're armed, too."

I took a chance and delivered that message with all the guts and glory I could muster. "Yeah," I said. "Good luck explaining the hippie in the back seat to those Mexican border guards. And they're armed, too."

Finally, 100 yards from the Mexican border, they pulled over on the freeway and opened the door. Not a word did they waste on me. Not a second did I waste in getting my scrawny, long-haired self out of that car.

I missed the first two periods of classes and arrived late to the third. I think I was lucky that day.

Another time Tom Moran and I hitchhiked from Monterrey to Coronado after a Transcendental Meditation retreat at Asilomar. We both had long ponytails and it was at night.

After three short rides, a fellow picked us up. He seemed in awe of our long hair. He told us he was drunk and asked if we wouldn't mind driving.

He crawled in the back seat and went to sleep. We drove until his car ran low on gas, then pulled over into a gas station, put a $20 bill on the dashboard with a thank-you note and continued on our journey.

Another time a man picked me up in Coronado. While driving over the bridge he began to have a seizure. As his hands tightened on the steering wheel and his mouth contorted in a painful manner, the car, at 60 mph, headed toward the center divider cones, spraying them every which way (before the concrete zipper was installed, they used 18-inch yellow plastic cones to manipulate commuter traffic on the bridge).

I managed to wrestle the wheel from his grasp and coasted to the off ramp near Chicano Park, where I leapt from the car and began to breathe again. Fortunately, I was on familiar ground, as many a time Lance Weber and I hitched over the bridge to the Barrio and La Popular, for rolled tacos, and then back home. It was pretty routine stuff in those days.

Nowadays, I doubt I'd pick up a hitchhiker under most circumstances. Maybe in daylight, if I could assess the person thoroughly before stopping, or deemed it an emergency. Cute girls, of course, were and are the exception.

But hitchhiking has gone the way of 8-tracks, Jimi Hendrix and the Cream; gone the way of wind wings, rain gutters and three-in-the-tree.

It's fun to look back on those years and those memories, and know I somehow endured them. By some assessments, I not only survived, but emerged out the other end a better man.

CHAPTER EIGHT

Transcendental Meditation & Beyond . . . (1970)

It must seem strange to people today. Hundreds of thousands of long-haired, drug-addled teenagers suddenly deciding "Timothy Leary is dead," praising a little man from India named Maharishi and trading in their drugs for a mantra.

Something parents, police and society couldn't accomplish, the Maharishi seemed to be doing with ease. That was the real end of the '60s, a seemingly forgotten, inward chapter that brought one era to a close and opened up the next.

Perhaps we took those years too seriously. Sure, we had developed bad habits. We lived by excesses, took shortcuts in life, and in fact, many just didn't come out of that era alive.

The previous mantra was, "Sex, Drugs, & Rock 'n' Roll." Nothing else seemed to matter, in what today's doctors would surely diagnose as a serious lack of frontal lobe development.

We lived in the moment. There was no tomorrow.

I remember driving by 601 First Street, here in Coronado. I'd be in a VW Beetle with my pals—Will Beauchamp, Dean Montunnas and

Mission San Luis Rey was the scene of a Transcendental Meditation retreat in the early 1970s. Hundreds of us turned out to learn more about this simple meditation technique that had radically changed our lives for the better. It was usually a long weekend, and we literally levitated back to Coronado after attending one of these. On this particular retreat, I was joined by good friends Jim Robeson and Steve Anderson. Photo by Steve Anderson.

Eddie Otero—smoking pot but slowing to watch a crowd of hippies and bikers file into that house.

"Yup," said Wilbur. "Looks like old Beulah babe is having another party."

"Let's go," I chirped from a cloud of smoke in the back seat.

"No, you can't go there," he said. "You have to go without smoking pot for a month. And you could never do that, Ditler."

Before long the Beach Boys and the Beatles began singing the praises of this little man with long hair and scraggly beard, who always wore a bed sheet, strands of beads and never brushed his hair.

He would be the opening act at many of their concerts and, believe me, it was a strange sight. It was a time of strange sights—Yoko Ono, Tiny Tim, the Maharishi.

The little man from India had a very high-pitched voice and spoke in a repetitive manner as he shared his concept for world peace, and a belief that if more people meditated, the world would be a better place—one meditator at a time.

The Maharishi was pretty certain we weren't going anywhere with our current lifestyle. You know what? He was right.

Something clicked inside me. On February 28, 1970, I had fulfilled my requirements of one-month drug- and drink-free.

I attended the required two introductory lectures and made an appointment to meet Beulah Smith, at her bay front home—601 First Street.

I arrived, per her instructions, with a white handkerchief, two pieces of fresh fruit and two flowers—oranges I bought at Free Brothers Market and roses I stole from Beulah's garden (if she knew, she never let on).

Within a few minutes, Beulah had settled me into a comfy chair and given me a mantra—an Indian Sanskrit word that had no meaning in our language.

Through that "sound," repeated over and over, I was able to transcend my conscious thinking level. The process was simple; my charming guide on this path patient. The rewards were beyond imagination.

And for the next decade and more, I greeted and ended each day of my life with a 20-minute meditation.

Three nights a week, Beulah opened her home to other meditators from around the county and we had group meditations. It was quite a colorful gathering in those early days—bikers, surfers, beat authors, musicians, Vietnam vets, bra-less earth mamas in tie-dye.

The word "trip"
took on an
entirely new meaning . . .

The smell of pot was replaced by incense; granola took the place of cheeseburgers; noise was defeated by inner silence. The word "trip" took on an entirely new meaning and yoga became a way of life.

Many will remember Beulah Smith and 601 First, but more so they will remember how she and the philosophies of her mentor, the Maharishi, led us out of the drug years and into the meditation years.

We quickly discovered we were using more of our minds doing this twice a day. But, most importantly, a spiritual path opened up that seemed to expose us all to a greater being, a greater energy; one that spoke no language or claimed no zip code or denomination. It would be decades before I finally figured out what that source, that energy, was, and my Christian faith has never been stronger.

Maharishi promised meditators they would one day reach a state of Cosmic Consciousness. That, he promised, would eventually lead to God Consciousness.

In the years to follow, each of us followed our own paths, but in Coronado alone, thousands of us used TM to guide us through the storms of our youth and into a better world.

Unbeknownst to me that day, Feb. 28, 1970, when Beulah led me into my new and healthier lifestyle, my father had coincidentally joined Alcoholics Anonymous. As we moved forward on our separate journeys, we developed the best relationship of our lives, and grew together in many wonderful ways. I'll always be grateful for that.

The Maharishi. I think if he hadn't had such a high-pitched voice and looked so cartoonish, he might have been taken more seriously by the masses. I met him once and sat at his feet with my friend Melanie Lococo at a Los Angeles lecture. The Maharishi and TM came at a good time. His teachings put a serious dent in the drug culture and saved a lot of lives, probably mine included.

Beulah Smith. She lived at 601 First Street and opened her bay view home to us three nights a week for group meditations. It was here I found my soul. Friends I made in those days are still in my life. Beulah was Maharishi's close friend and first instructor in the United States. What a lovely woman she was.

Not two months after my initiation to TM, however, I was invited on a Mexico trip with Paul Free, Mike McCartin and Denny McNeilage. We drove Paul's Ford van down to San Felipe, then we took on the hideous rocky road to Puertocitos.

While there, we fished and dove, built huge campfires and just sort of rediscovered ourselves under the most amazing canopy of stars and constellations. Fresh fish breakfast, lunch and dinner.

One night a *chubasco* blew in with winds of 100 mph. There was nowhere to go, nowhere to hide, so we each found a large tombstone-like rock and crawled into our sleeping bags on the lee side of the storm.

The next morning we had to dig out, as we were covered with sand and shells. The van was on its side. And there was Paul, sitting atop the driver's door, trying to get an 8-track tape to play. It was the Beatles' "Abby Road" album, and he was cueing it to the song, "Here Comes the Sun." Can't hear that song today without remembering that morning on the beach in the aftermath of a *chubasco* that had destroyed nearby San Felipe.

Down the beach was another campsite. Two families and their daughters. One of the girls and I had taken a fancy to each other (must have been my long hair) and did a lot of walking and talking along those starry nights and deserted Mexican beaches.

She wanted me to get stoned with her, but I explained I was on a different trip, an inward journey that didn't involve external stimuli such as drugs and alcohol.

When we left, she gave me this huge joint as a parting gift. I figured I'd just be polite and take it, then give it away stateside to one of my stoner friends.

As we drove through the border in Tijuana, they pulled us into Secondary. They tore that van apart completely. They had us strip. I had stored the joint in my sock. "C'mon boy, I said everything," said the agent. As he turned to write something down, I popped that thick-as-your-thumb, four-inch joint in my mouth and began to chew. Agh. It was so dry and so awful, and so big.

The border agent turned and started to laugh. He had pity on me and gave me some water. He laughed and said, "Oh, well, I guess if that's all you had we're okay."

As we drove up the 5 freeway in that van, with wall and ceiling panels falling on us and screws popping out, I suddenly came on to that joint. Boy did I feel stupid at that point. The reluctant stoner.

Well, it didn't faze me or deter me from my path to enlightenment, as Beulah would call it. I meditated for many years and lived the better and healthier lifestyle because of it.

Even now, before I get my blood pressure tested, I sit for a moment and recall my mantra. Immediately my breathing relaxes, the wrinkles smooth out on my forehead and my blood pressure drops.

I don't meditate much these days, but the entire experience left me with a spiritual appreciation that rings true today. It gave me a God experience that has changed everything in my life, for the better, and put me on a list that begins with the word, "Survivor."

***

"Kidnapping in the Name of God"

Distractions and temptations were everywhere. Shortly after beginning TM, while attending Southwestern Junior College, I struggled with what to take, what my major might be, what I wanted to be when I "grew up."

All of that could be another book, but suffice to say I started out as a psychology major. The encounter groups alone from that year would make for tremendous reading—how we all coped with our issues as a group of 30-plus young students, guarded over by a teacher, Elwyn Wong, who guided us through all the highs and lows of those gatherings.

But in all seriousness, I have wonderful memories from those weekly encounter groups. They, just like that first-generation rock 'n' roll, and the introspective LSD trips of years prior, were all a part of the twilight of the "Summer of Love."

As I say, I was a psychology major that year (1970). Then, I fell in love with a girl in the art department. The next year I was an art major.

One afternoon, after practice on the tennis team, my friends and I, along with my artist girlfriend Vickie, sat along the undeveloped ridge of land above the tennis courts.

My friend Malcolm had a guitar. He was a long-haired Latino fellow I had grown close to at Southwestern. Handsome devil, funny, but perhaps not the sharpest pencil in the box.

We built a fire and were enjoying the October sunset, which I soon began to refer to as Indian summer. I still do to this day. It's especially wonderful, as it was that night, when the warm Santa Ana winds begin to blow.

A converted school bus pulled up. Out of it came the most attractive people you could imagine. There were guys with long hair, wearing

The everlasting Steve Anderson. I don't think I can share half the adventures we had together. He is now a professional photographer on the music scene. We are still good friends and somehow manage an adventure now and then together.

tie-dyed T-shirts. They had guitars and other hand-held instruments, and the most spellbinding smiles I'd ever seen.

. . . handles such as Bambi, Pebbles, Asia and Domino.

The women were young and beautiful, with long hair flowing wildly, flowers tucked behind their ears. They scarcely wore anything, and certainly no bras. They mingled quickly with us, hugging and telling us their first names—many of which were handles such as Bambi, Pebbles, Asia and Domino.

Vickie was quickly befriended by them as we sat and played music. They had brought some delightful food items, which didn't last long at all. Then, as it started to grow dark, they asked us all to hop on the bus and join them at their mansion in Mission Hills, where they were preparing a huge turkey dinner and, as they assured us, the really good musicians in their group were waiting, already warming up their instruments.

Malcomb and Vickie jumped on the bus despite my warnings not to.

My best friend at the time was Steve Anderson, another Coronado boy—a Navy brat, son of a preacher. Steve got the address and said he would drive over later. Thankfully that was not his intention, but they bought his story and wrote down their address.

We returned to Coronado to compare notes. From what little we had gotten in the fractured conversations around the fire, they called themselves "Children of God." We wouldn't find out until years later what a vicious cult they were and how much damage they had inflicted on unsuspecting youth.

Steve, of course, had a plan. "Let's hop in your station wagon, sneak up on the place and steal Vickie and Malcomb back." At the time I was still driving my 1961 Ford ranch wagon—a station wagon with two doors, a tailgate, lots of secret compartments and a column stick shift that loudly kicked out of first gear before you were ready.

Steve lived in a little two-bedroom shack behind the laundromat on Orange, across the street from Cora-Mart. In his guest room, which he called the Pubic Room, long pink ribbons hung from a red ceiling light and fan. As I recall there was a waterbed under all of that mess.

The place had been rented for ages by one class of UDT (Underwater Demolition Team—the early Navy frogmen and precursor to Navy SEALs) after another. The damage from their many keg parties had left the place barely standing, but to Steve it was home, a very affordable home.

As we ran out the front door to my car, Steve yelled, "Wait!" He ran back inside and came out with this book called, of all things, "Satin's Bible." "We'll need this," he shouted.

I cringed, but there was no time for questions. We raced over to Mission Hills and the large house we later learned the Children of God stole from an old gentleman who had mysteriously disappeared.

It was dark on the outside, but we could see light coming through shuttered windows of a few rooms. We went to the rear of the house and found an unlocked kitchen door.

As we went in, a beautiful couple smiled at us and welcomed us. They, of course, split us up. Steve was walked down a long hall. I was put in a room with about 15 people my age, all sitting around an older fellow who was reading and chanting.

I didn't see Vickie so I tried to leave. Surprise, surprise, the door handles had been removed from inside the room. Fortunately, Steve arrived a moment later and let me out.

As we explored each room in the house, we finally found Vickie and Malcomb. We acted as though we were part of the "family" and smiled big, floated instead of walked, and in general acted as though we had just dropped some powerful acid, in an attempt to look like the rest of those lost sheep.

I never saw him again . . .

We led Vickie out of the room but Malcomb resisted. He was a big boy, so we didn't want to make too much of a scene. I never saw him again after that.

As we went through the front door, Vickie suddenly snapped out of her condition and began to fight me like a crazy woman. I tried to explain that she was being held against her will, but she insisted I was wrong.

Just as we approached my car, which I had parked a couple of blocks away behind a large hedge, three men burst through the front door of the house in pursuit.

Neither Steve nor I have a good explanation for what happened next. He yelled, "Go, get her in the car and start the engine. I'll be there." He then pulled out that book he had been carrying, "Satin's Bible." He held it up in front of the three pursuers and they stopped dead in their tracks. Now, you've got to understand, I wasn't a fully developed Christian at that point in my life, but I knew God was good and the devil not so good.

Steve's book had them paralyzed. To this day I can't explain it, but it gave us just the time we needed to make our escape

I got Vickie in the car and started the engine. Just as she was about to open the door and jump out, Steve jumped in and pinned her between us in the front seat—a bench seat. This was, of course, pre-seatbelts.

We flew down the road as my transmission loudly popped out of first gear sounding like a shotgun blast. As we passed the house, there must have been 20 or more of those Children of God slapping the car, grabbing at the door handles, trying to stop us.

We made it back to Coronado and decided it was best if we all stayed at Steve's place that night, then drive Vickie back to her home in Chula Vista the next morning.

Well, Vickie and I ended up sleeping in the Pubic Room, but we slept well. That next morning her fight had diminished, but she was extremely upset at what we had done. She continued to tell me how wonderful they were to her, and how she wanted to go back.

I drove her home and explained to her parents what had happened. Her father was an art professor of mine the prior year and, fortunately, we had forged a brief relationship. They were skeptical but grateful. They soon realized how serious her plight had been, and expressed much gratitude to us in the weeks that followed. Vickie never spoke to me again, but I understand she got her life back, married and had a ton of kids.

What we all found out in the months to come was that the Children of God was a nationwide cult that used group hypnosis and mild drugs in the food and drink to weaken the resolve of their new recruits.

Steve, who had been teasing me mercilessly about my meditating, enrolled in a TM lecture series immediately afterward, got his mantra and had many pleasant years of transcending the realities of life, such as they were. We had a lot of fun together in those early years. We still get together occasionally for a Neil Young or Stephen Stills concert or a good surf.

Years later Governor Reagan appointed a well-known attorney, Ted

Patrick, to investigate the Children of God. That poor fellow ended up in prison for doing the same thing we did for Vickie. Only, in his case, the young lady he rescued sued him for kidnapping her against her will and won.

All of this, of course, only reinforced my feelings that drugs had no place in my future as I continued my life with Transcendental Meditation, yoga, and eventually Christianity.

Indeed, my meditations have been replaced with prayer, but sometimes, in the quiet of the night, I can still hear Beulah as she softly brought us out of our meditations with those three little words, "Jai Guru Dev."

CHAPTER NINE

The VW Bus
(1971)

I had no idea how cold 50° below zero could be, or how shitty the heaters were in VW busses. It was a hasty decision to accept Dean Montunnas's invite to visit. He and his brother Gary lived in Park City, Utah, and at a time when it was still a one-VW town.

It was at a period in my life after high school, in the middle of an on-and off-again relationship with Southwestern Junior College, and I was just craving something new in my life. Before I gave it a whole lot of thought, I had loaded up my van with food and gas, and headed to Utah.

Fortunately, some other friends (John Setter and Steve Cooley) were headed to Salt Lake City, so we caravanned. That came in handy as we crossed the desert and one thing after another broke on our cars. Misery loves company, and Steve was handy with a wrench.

Our first stop was to visit the Carter brothers—Lane and Gary. They, it seemed, had carved out a special little niche for themselves amongst the staid Mormon families in their neighborhood.

As best we could tell, they were the only long-haired, guitar-playing California boys within 100 miles. I'll never forget pulling up in front

In the early-mid 1960s, the streets of Coronado were familiar roadways for these blue VW busses. They traveled in a caravan, whether it be to high school, to the beach, surfing or camping, or wherever their cars would lead them. Photo courtesy Bruce and Clarence Muirhead.

of their house. The garage door was open and the Carter brothers were jamming on guitar and harmonica. There must have been a dozen young Mormon girls discovering their hippie selves that day—shaking and swaying to and fro, ogling Lane and Gary as though they were rock legends.

We stayed the weekend, and then I headed off to find the Montunnas brothers. When I found them, they were living in a Park City trailer home and nearly starving. No one was working.

Gary, the older brother, had this plan that we would hitchhike to the Virgin Islands, where he was certain we could homestead land. We were all meditators in those days, so we spent a lot of time starting and ending the day with Transcendental Meditation. Meanwhile, outside, the thermometer was dropping. It got to 50 below zero on my second night there.

It was 1970 and I was at that "I know it all" age of 20. I had a phony ID saying I was 23, and Dean and I hit every bar and restaurant in Park City looking for work.

100

Back then Park City was the only ski resort on the mountain, and the biggest event occurred on Saturday night, when everyone piled into an old barn to watch "War of the Worlds." The film was shown on a bed sheet tacked to the wall. We sat on straw and drank red wine and whisky. The real manger scene maybe didn't have cows and goats, but we sure did.

The sign in the town's favorite bar said, "Boneless Chicken: 50 cents." The joke was on me as I flipped my last two quarters at the bartender and he flipped a hardboiled egg back at me.

Half frozen, long-haired and smelling like a dairy farm . . .

It was so cold that winter we had to place Sterno burners under the oil pan of Dean's VW bus to thin the oil before we could start the engine. Then, we had to load his neighbor's two goats into the back of the bus to create extra body warmth.

It's no wonder we never found a job. Half frozen, long-haired and smelling like a dairy farm, we walked into every business in town seeking work.

After a month of that, while visiting the library in Salt Lake City, I discovered Gary's plan for homesteading the Virgin Islands was based on an out-of-date *Encyclopedia Britannica*.

It seems the Rockefellers had purchased all of that land two years earlier, and the last thing they wanted was a bunch of California hippies camping on their land.

"Broke, busted, disgusted, Gary can't be trusted, and Ditler wants to go to the sea . . ."

So I fired up my old van and, with the help of three Mormon sister wives (and their coffee tin full of gas money), I made my way back to Coronado.

I dropped them off at a relative's home in Las Vegas and stayed the night. No, you don't get that story here. Besides, this is a story about VW busses.

That's me, years after the adventures described in this book, still with a bad case of VW bus envy. Photo by Chelsea Ditler.

The VW bus. Was there ever a more universally comfortable vehicle? Some were painted a single color; many were two-toned; some had flowers on the side; but, in Coronado, most just had surfboards on the roof or sticking out the rear.

Car cosmetics were not something we gave a damn about. And no matter how steep the incline, or how heavy the load, a VW bus could climb anything in low gear. Maybe not fast, but slow and steady was the rule of the day when driving them.

When pulling into the Palm Springs "End of the World" Pop Festival, I saw a beautiful VW bus with an unfinished cubist painting of Jimi Hendrix across the front. In my altered state of mind, I quickly completed the image as we drifted off to the music of John Mayall and the Bluesbreakers.

Scoops on the sides, bubbles on top, windows folded out, a four- or eight-track tape player under the dash, curtains drawn.

If this bus is a rockin' don't come a knockin'. Or, as my friend Denise once said to me, "My mother would never let me date anyone who drove a VW bus."

Regardless of the year, or the number of windows, whether you bought it new, or were the 9th owner, the VW bus was a kingdom on wheels.

Salt sea air seemed to turn paint to rust overnight, and the side windows were far too easy to break into. The necker knob on the steering wheel got a lot of use, and I still find myself hypnotized by the sound of downshifting a VW. I still turn my head with anticipation at the sound of a VW engine puttering by. It's something I'll never forget.

There was something special about the way they rode across dips, the way I collapsed over the steering wheel and steered with my elbows and forearms. Looking back, the VW bus was the most enjoyable car I've ever driven.

Many a time a stick of rose incense from Oriental Imports was wedged into the Blaupunkt dashboard speaker in an attempt to disguise what was being smoked in the backseat.

Jim Robeson had a cherry VW bus. Often, he and I would sit in his bus at Officer's Beach, on North Island. His dad was military, so we just drove right on to the base to check the surf, or, in some cases, to smoke a joint undisturbed by civilian traffic.

"Get out of the car with your hands up."

My brief effort to depart Coronado involved a trip to Park City, Utah. It was so cold we had to put Sterno canned heat burners under the oil pan of the VW bus and wait until the oil was thin enough for the engine to start. Then, we loaded goats into the back so we would have some body warmth as we drove around that little one-horse town (as it was then) looking for jobs. How cold was it? One night it dropped to 50 below zero.

Boneless chicken was a bad joke. When I walked off that cold and snowy Park City street, into this little bar that still had hitching posts for horses out front, I only saw the sign. The bartender took my last two quarters and flipped me a hardboiled egg. Sustenance? Sure. But far from what my taste buds envisioned upon reading that sign.

Once, after we had chucked our bad habits and rolling papers, and turned to meditation for our high, we were sitting in that spot meditating. Like I said, the rose incense was burning and we were deep, deep into our transcendent freefalls.

Then, all of a sudden, we hear over a loudspeaker, "Get out of the car with your hands up."

The base security thought we were smoking pot. Can you imagine? Us? Well, they missed that opportunity by a year or more, and boy, were we glad they did. Jim's father was called, but eventually they let us go.

Returning from surf trips to Mexico, it was commonplace to have surfboards wedged in the back, stinky wetsuits between the boards so as not to ruin the wax bead.

Girlfriends lay on top of all that, and coming across the border no one would ever guess a kilo of marijuana was hidden away at the very bottom, or bottles of tequila and Kahlúa stashed under the seats.

The border guard questions were always the same: "Where were you born? What's your business? Are you bringing anything back across the border?"

VW memories. They're everywhere. I remember Buddy Jordan blowing up the engine in his bus while driving down the Strand one night. He was so stoned, and laughing so hard, that he forgot to shift out of second gear.

Behind Cora-Mart, on any given day, you could find Lance Weber at the Yellow House, up to his elbows in grease, either dropping a dead VW engine or putting a rebuilt one back in.

Lance kept a lot of VWs on the road in those days. It wasn't as profitable as drug smuggling, but then again, the risks were far less.

Or Mitch Bucklew, tooling down the Strand in his Lance Weber-modified VW panel bus. An eager young sailor in a souped-up Mustang passed in the fast lane, revving his engines just to remind us who was the tortoise and who was the hare.

"Hang on," Buck would yell, as he unleashed the Corvette engine sitting amidships in his bus, leaving the Mustang in the dust and a look of disbelief on the face of the swab driving it. We went so fast that, had that bus had wings, we would've been airborne in a matter of seconds.

Parking alongside the beach with the side doors open meant we were holding court. Anyone (and everyone) dropped in to share the moment. Dave Chalmers' bus was usually our headquarters at Center Beach after a good surf session. There was so much smoke coming out of the open doors anyone looking in had trouble seeing who was sitting inside, not that it really mattered.

They could pick out voices. If the talk was of twin fins, it was usually Mike Coleman. If it was of the perfect wave it was probably Kevin Curtis. If it was about sleeping with that gorgeous blonde at the Hotel Del the night before, it was Jimmy Reilly or Bob Lahodny.

I remember Ron and Kathy Clark parking their VW bus along the bay to steal a kiss whenever the urge hit. They had just come through rocky divorces, and had found each other. What a love affair they had. We lost Ron and Kathy a few years back. I sure miss them. Coronado Royalty, for sure.

Then there was obstinate and arrogant Jeff Montunnas, the middle brother, holding court in the back seat of his VW as a stable of impressionable young drivers took turns chauffeuring him around town.

He had lost his driver's license but wasn't about to give up his VW bus.

Or Stephanie Aston-Jones' red-and-white VW bus. She personified the cute hippie babe down the street. She was my friend Skip's older sister, so I had plenty of time to sit and gawk at her. Last year I finally confessed to her about my high school crush on her. I think she was flattered, even though it took me 45 years to get up the nerve. Of course, I also had crushes on her classmates, Tori Curtis and Jeanne Riley. I had and still have a love affair with the Class of '68.

After Stephanie sold that bus, it sat in the lot at Rose Ford (where Park Place Liquor is today). I would climb in after the store closed, sit behind the wheel, turn on the AM radio to KCBQ and listen to the Doors, imagining this special old bus was mine.

Such was the effect the VW bus had on us. It was a happy time . . . it was our time.

CHAPTER TEN

Coronado's Outlaw Bike Races (1970–1974)

I t's hard to believe now, looking back, how crazy we were growing up in Coronado. Of course, every generation will lay claim to a certain degree of extremism in their youth, but this one really pushed the limits.

Perhaps the story that best represents our generation involved the Outlaw Bike Races of 1970-1974. Some of you will deny those years (especially when your children are in the room) others will embrace them.

These weren't really races per se. They were more like survival outings that involved bicycles, underage kids, lots of beer and a hot Sunday afternoon in a much older and less politically correct Coronado.

There were tragedies. There were poor choices made. But there was also fun to be had. It was "Little Rascals" meets "Hells Angels," and some of those old memories continue to glow warmly in our minds.

This story begins one spring day in 1971 as Coronado police stopped traffic on Orange Avenue to allow 400 screaming, summer-ready teenagers to cross from Ocean Boulevard in a massive wave of bicycles, long hair and skin. We flew across Coronado's sedate main street like a swarm of gooney birds. I can still remember the looks on the faces of drivers in cars, stopped by uniformed police officers, and wondering what the heck was going on.

"Those were the beer races," recalled former cop Bob Paseman. "The first race was utter confusion. No one knew what the bike racers were going to do next, or where they were headed.

"At first we tried to correct the problem, but we were outnumbered 200-to-one," said Paseman, who never wearies of waxing reminiscent whenever three or more of us are gathered. "We arrested a few in an attempt to put a stop to it, but to no avail. Finally, we just gave up."

I know that Paseman's stories about me continue to grow with each telling. So much so that even I'm not sure where fact ends and fiction begins. But, all these years later, it's in good fun, and we all participate in the conversations, each trying to impress the other with memories, anecdotes and long-forgotten names. If someone had told me then I would one day be best friends with Officer Paseman, I would have scoffed.

Although beer-fueled bike races were held in Coronado dating back to the late 1950s (in those days they actually were races, although involving just a few guys, lots of beer, and usually bloody crashes somewhere along the route), the town had never seen anything like the outlaw races of the 1970s.

The organizers for the outlaw bike races were young and catered to the younger. We had total disregard for the law. I got started down that road when some of the older generation—Jim Newhall, Bill Gise and others—were staging one of their bike races and a stop on Orange Avenue looked inviting.

"And get a haircut . . ."

I entered the yard, opened a can of beer, and was promptly lifted high over the head of Bob Addy. He and Jim Darnell proceeded to throw me over a hedge onto the sidewalk with the message, "Come back when you're twenty-one, kid," said Addy. "And get a haircut," said Darnell.

On that day, I decided to create my own brand of bike race, only my rules were different. My first rule was, "No one OVER the age of 21

As word spread that the bike race was about to start, another hundred people flowed out into the alley. No one dared get between the leaders and the next stop. Nearly a third of these "innocent" teens would fail to reach the final stop, but to this day they wear their adventures, crashes and all, on their chest proudly, and their tales of the Outlaw Bike Races grow with each passing year.

The late, great Lance Weber, leading the pack on his latest bicycle creation. Towards the back of the pack they knew to just follow that British flag. The group is seen here traveling down Pomona Avenue.

can enter this bike race." I co-authored four of them before the social and political climate in Coronado prevented them from continuing any longer.

The older guys, the founders of the original bike races, were largely made up of off-duty cops and firemen. They met in deserted dirt lots (there were many empty lots in Coronado in those days). They had T-shirts made, everyone rode two-by-two while paying attention to traffic laws, and they followed their leader from stop to stop.

Obviously, that didn't appeal to me and my friends. Our rules were simple, but different. Each race had a gauntlet of six stops (large, glamorous homes in various parts of Coronado, scheduled on dates when the parents were out of town).

At first, we went the route of cans of beer in buckets of ice, but my partner, Lance Weber, was one of those genius types. He was always on the lookout for a better way to do things.

Lance came up with the idea of using jockeyboxes—large aluminum boxes filled with ice, and fitted with four rapid-pour nozzles. We proudly advertised six kegs of beer at each stop. With six stops, that's 36 kegs of beer. We split it down the middle—three lite, three dark at each stop. You can do the math, but it adds up to one heck of a lot of beer.

Copper tubing went from the kegs of beer, through the tubing, through the ice, and, then driven by CO_2, came out the beer nozzles fast, icy cold and with no foam.

Anyone who has ever stood around a keg with people lined up screaming for a beer, knows the frustration—pumping the handle, holding the skinny hose in one hand while trying to fill a flimsy beer cup in the other, beer dribbling out the hose slow, warm and foamy, as opposed to fast, cold and foamless.

People suddenly were drinking far more than one or two cans of beer at each stop. And, no, we never paused to consider the consequences of that much beer on young bodies and minds until years later.

One problem that has always plagued the outlaw bike races was keeping people out who didn't pay. Not until the final of the four races did Lance come up with a solution. He purchased an industrial sized bag of these new-fangled things called "zip ties."

As kids lined up with their money at the first stop, he would zip a tie on their wrist. That made it easy to determine who paid and who crashed the party at a glance.

Unfortunately, Lance got carried away with himself and zipped them too tight. By the third stop wrists were going numb and colorless and fingers stopped working. But, we had larger fish to fry by the third stop, as you'll see.

The location of the stops was the best-kept secret, known only to the race organizers. If word got out that someone's house was to be a stop, that house was removed at the last minute and substituted with another. Should such a violation of our agreement take place, the violator was disgraced amongst his or her friends. On the other hand, if someone's house was a bike-race stop, that person's status grew immensely among his or her island peers.

Two-page spread: *By the time we dropped down into the Flats, residents fled inside their homes all along the length of Margarita. Lance Weber can be seen in the middle of the pack, moving at a slower pace to accommodate the amount of beer his many young charges had consumed at that point. Photo by Donnie Woodhouse.*

What took place at the stops ran the gamut. It didn't take long for people to realize they couldn't let bike race participants use the restrooms in their parents' large, luxurious homes. That proved to be utter chaos. So, when they saw the bicycles coming around the corner, they locked their doors, confining the sweeping army of racers to the yards.

When you drink that much beer, there is only one constant. You HAVE to pee. Consequently, people began seeking places to pee, men and women—bushes, trees, rose gardens, the neighbor's backyard, between parked cars. They say water has a way of finding its way. Well, so does pee, or at least those needing to do so.

Bike race organizers used to make bets to see who could get "lucky"

the most times during the course of one day's bike race. The races lasted from 10 or 11 a.m. until dark. And, yes, there was a lot of sex taking place. There was also a lot of passing out. It was not uncommon to see your surfing buddies, wearing nothing but ragged and beer-stained canvas shorts, passed out in the bushes, legs sticking out. The surf shorts back then were built to withstand wipeouts in the water, but not on land.

Our predecessors, the "adult" bike racers, used to stage wet T-shirt contests at the end of their races. We never did that, but we did have some nudity.

The older bike racers also did what they called a "Muff-Race," where the braless female lifted her shirt over the male's head while he lifted her up off the ground. With her legs tightly wrapped around his torso, and blinded by, well, blinded by her assets, she tried to instruct her partner

This is one of those photos everyone loves. Many of the people in this shot are still alive. In this photo, they range from 15-18 years of age. No wonder they all treat me with such affection nearly half a century later. Nobody else in their little world would let them get this crazy. Photo by Caroline Haines.

in navigating obstacles on the ground on the way to a finish line. I think the winner got a case of Pabst Blue Ribbon.

One of the adult bike racers knocked two holes in the single-wall construction of his garage at one of the stops. Women lined up on the other side and stuck their bare breasts through the holes.

Without knowing who the contestants were, bike race officials stood on the other side with black Sharpies, contemplated the competition, and marked the breasts 1-10, 10 being the most perfect. I don't remember what the first-place contestant won, but I recall her showing off her "score." Funny, but looking back at that, our outlaw bike races seem tame in comparison.

Meanwhile, the local police went nuts trying to anticipate what was going to happen next. "Our only recourse was to assist the outlaw bike racers in crossing streets to prevent accidents," said Officer Paseman, "and let them proceed to their next secret stop. Periodically, we would pick up stragglers and try to pry information out of them, but nobody would or could talk."

The next year I very cautiously shared the route of bike race stops with the Coronado Police Department. It turned out to be a good thing, as the police went ahead of us stopping traffic at all major intersections. It was a match made in hell, but it worked to everyone's benefit.

It was a relationship born on the field of battle.

Officer Bill Arbuckle, a great guy, simply asked me to use the roof speaker on one of their police cars, usually reserved for crowd control, to request that participants move their bikes from the alley so traffic could get by. It was a relationship born on the field of battle. Now, having said that, if Officer Clardy had asked me, I would have flipped him the bird and walked away.

There were some awfully friendly cops in those days, such as Happenstall, Arbuckle, O'Hara, Crook, Dodson, Miller, Grimaud, and, of course, Paseman, all who would give us a short lecture and drive us home, rather than book us for drinking beer behind the pool with our girlfriends or crashing our dad's car on the Strand. Of course, there were the angry and overzealous cops, too, some of whom were just plain mean—Clardy, Soto, Datson, Stolpe, Hodges, Jury, Black.

We knew all of them, and they knew all of us. It was a different time in Coronado. Most of them lived on the island, so we saw them in the neighborhood, at the store, etc. Some, like Bob Paseman and Denny Grimaud, started out with power-driven agendas and mellowed over the years.

The patience of those good cops was severely tested, however, as entering the Coronado bike race was an endurance game of the most unbelievable magnitude.

"My fondest memory of the bike races is sneaking in at age fifteen," recalled Corinne Baldauf, now a successful corporate executive, "and reprising the Woodstock chant 'Na na na na nahhhh' as we were riding. I remember skinned knees and hanging onto my cup, which became more precious with every stop."

Unlike our color-coordinated predecessors, we were half naked. The guys usually wore surf trunks. The girls usually just wore bikinis. Everyone's hair was wild and, looking back at photos of those early bike races, that was some kinda brotherhood and sisterhood we had back then—friendships that survive even now, nearly half a century later.

One of the toughest challenges at the Coronado Bike Race was keeping 300 to 400 people grouped together in one lane while traveling between stops. Everyone wanted to ride at the front of the pack and bikes would often spread out over both lanes and the sidewalks.

Terry Bucklew had a trick to deal with that. In 1969, just weeks after the bridge had opened, we would lead the unsuspecting bike riders up the apron of the bridge, cranking a U-turn just before we got to the ticket booths. Uniformed ticket takers would run out in a panic, waving their arms, trying to stop us. It was quite a sight, and it usually caused the masses behind us to thin out into a narrower stream of chaos for the next few blocks.

What goes in, must come out. As owners of the bike race-stop homes got wise to flooded and trashed bathrooms, doors became locked, forcing men and women to be creative in where they peed. Participants had to consume six full-sized kegs of beer at each stop, making sights such as this one commonplace on bike race day.

Lance and I had a different approach. When the group began to bulge (usually after the third stop and a few too many beers), we would head the group down Ocean Boulevard and implement this technique we dreamed up for thinning out the crowd. Heading toward North Beach, we would turn without warning into what was known as "Crazy Alley" (between Pine Street and Ocean Drive).

Unlike our predecessors, who rode ten-speed bikes with curl-down handlebars, most of our riders were on beach cruisers. A typical beach cruiser was fitted out with ape hanger handlebars nearly as wide as the bike was long. They sported large, cushioned, or banana, seats. They had one speed and sometimes no brakes. As riders tried to make the turn into Crazy Alley, they would be forced into wooden fences on either side like a group of longhorn steers being herded into the chute.

As strips of wooden fencing fell to the onslaught of this runaway pack of bicyclists, people either had to drop back in line or crash. It was a splintery disaster that no one enjoyed, but it was successful in temporarily thinning out the vanguard and giving the leaders room to maneuver. Belated apologies to the residents of that alley, who were forever replacing wooden strips in their fences.

"It's hard to believe that was so long ago," said my best friend, the late Mitch Sanders. He was a local firefighter who participated in the outlaw races as a teenager. "It was funny and carefree to us then. Once I became a parent and a homeowner, I realized what a terror we must have been to the older residents of the island, not to mention to our parents."

Mitch was one of my lieutenants, along with little Petey Johnson. They would help prepare the stops, carry the heavy beer kegs and hardware from stop to stop, and in general enjoy the fame of being a "bike race organizer." You'll have to ask them about the perks of such an envious title.

Bud Bernhard, the legendary recluse and brick layer, took over that job the final two years, stealthily moving the equipment through a network of alleyways, out of sight of the masses, and having everything ready when the eager army of bicyclists arrived at the next stop.

People would arrive at each stop with all the enthusiasm of miners jumping off the ship and headed for Sutter's Mill. Only it wasn't "Gold!" they were yelling, it was "Beer!!!" They would pull up on their bikes, break ranks from the group, ride their bikes into bushes or walls. No kickstands. No bike locks. In fact, few finished on the bike they started with.

Underway, between bike race stops, the crashes were legendary and are still talked about. Fallen riders were usually up and moving within seconds for fear of losing sight of the pack, and inevitably not knowing where the next stop was. Such was our ability to keep the route secret.

It was a horrendous sight—elbows and knees bloodied, broken spokes sticking out from bent rims, handlebars twisted, and everyone looking

Photos on this page and next courtesy Jim Newhall.

a little shell-shocked. The only good news was that, as mentioned, they were probably riding someone else's bike, as they couldn't find their own as the last stop approached and the day wound down.

One year, while riding along Ocean Boulevard., a fellow rode up and untied the bikini top on a well-endowed young woman. (Lisa, I'll spare your last name from this story.) Before the bathing suit hit the ground so did 60 bikers. We heard the crash way up at the front of the pack, around F and Tolita. We turned around, wanting to help, but it was obvious the only thing we could do was keep going.

> *. . . wheels wobbling,*
> *spokes twanging,*
> *blood flowing . . .*

"They will find a way to follow JD," said my co-conspirator Lance with sage confidence. And indeed, they did—wheels wobbling, spokes twanging, blood flowing but everyone smiling and doing their best to limp along behind us and stay within sight of the pack.

One year, the late Jimmy Reilly was riding on the sidewalk with no

hands between stops four and five, when he was suddenly introduced to a tree limb that knocked him cold. He was taken to Coronado Hospital.

"I couldn't believe all the people being brought in," Reilly told me at the time, "and all from the bike race. While waiting for our folks to pick us up, we compared war wounds and shared stories.

"One guy had hit a parking meter and cracked a rib," said Reilly. "Another was found head first in the back seat of a Thunderbird convertible over on Country Club Lane—feet sticking up in the air." His handlebars made short work of the T-Bird's new soft top.

The final race in 1974 ended at 1026 G Avenue, the Haley house. An unsuspecting neighbor looked out her window, horrified to see a group of young men desecrating her roses.

The aggrieved family had done their homework. They told the *Coronado Journal* how the bike race "started at 1411 Seventh Street, followed by more beer drinking." They verified the racers had also stopped at 135 H, 1011 E and 963 I avenues, with a very lengthy stop at 1156 Isabella Avenue (Ernesto Vasquez's home) that included a rare "bike race intermission" designed to let us jump in the ocean and temporarily sober up.

The local newspaper reported that the city manager and police chief had been publicly accused of dereliction of duty in mishandling the bike race.

In the end, and despite the involvement of the district attorney, the city council, the California Dept. of Alcoholic Beverage Control and a handful of attorneys, no action was taken because the witness wasn't able to identify the perpetrators who desecrated her rose garden. Someone suggested she wasn't looking at their faces.

After that final race, I threw my bike in the back of my van and sought refuge at Steve Anderson's in Mission Beach, along the boardwalk. For the next week I stayed with him, afraid to return to Coronado for fear I'd be arrested.

That final race in 1974 awakened to the dawn of the age of litigation. It was to be the last of the outlaw bike races, but not before a memorable third stop at the Haines house on E Avenue. Sisters Pam, Caroline and Bunny pleaded with us to let them be a bike race stop, even though their backyard was small. They insisted their older brother was out of town, their mother was on a travel junket, and their father was commanding a research vessel in the South Pacific. "There's no way we'll get caught," said Pammy Haines.

It so happened we lost a stop at the last minute, so the Haines' house was added. Everything went well until half way through the beer. Pam came running out of the house screaming, "My dad is at the airport and headed home. Everyone, get out of here NOW!"

We worked like clockwork to implement crisis control and move the beer, clean the yard, and get people on the road to the fourth stop. But as we were preparing to leave, someone found an 11-year-old neighbor boy passed out in the yard. Seems he had sneaked in and had some beer.

In our haste, we decided to just cover him with fallen leaves from the trees. He would wake up later and no one would know.

Bob "Baines" Haines," whom we loved dearly, came home, lit a cigar and began to rake his yard. It's said the neighbors two blocks away could hear him yelling when he found that poor kid buried under the leaves. Now, almost half a century later, he has forgiven his daughters, and forgiven me, thankfully. Still, I fully expect some grown man to walk up to me one day and tell me he was that little boy. I figure he must be about 58 by now.

"Overall, the kids had a good time and it was an experience for everyone involved," said Officer Paseman. "It was a time when things were simpler, people were more relaxed, and the younger generation had a good rapport with the police and the community. That could never happen these days."

Today those young and reckless riders have grown to become successful lawyers, doctors, pilots, SEALs, restaurant owners, contractors, filmmakers, politicians and bankers with families of their own. Many even have grandchildren.

The Coronado Bike Races, and in particular the outlaw bike races, may be forever lost to Coronado history, and while many remember that era fondly, others would gladly say, "Thank God we made it through those years."

The history of Coronado's bike races is far larger than these four outlaw races. The outlaw races were just an offshoot of a much larger legacy. Another time, another place, that story will hopefully see the light of day, but for now, I thank Bill Gise and Jim Newhall for opening their photo archive to me. More than that, I thank them for forgiving us for making their legitimate bike races, and their lives, miserable for a few years way back when our mental development was still in its infancy.

CHAPTER ELEVEN

The Chowder House Marching Kazoo Band (1972)

Seventy thousand people lined Coronado's Orange Avenue in 1972. It was the annual July Fourth Parade—a tradition that had been carried out, on and off, since 1888, and had always involved a mass exodus of people from San Diego to our shores.

Standing, sitting and sleeping on the corner yards of First Street and D Avenue, I was surrounded by a group of serape-clad teenagers with large sombreros—most coping with the residual effects of too much beer and tequila the night before.

It looked like a scene from a Sergio Leone Spaghetti Western. There is no evidence to confirm ownership of the empty tequila bottle sitting on the grass, but our group of rag-tag youth definitely understood how "fiesta" led to "siesta."

Dressed in white muslin pants, white Mexican wedding shirts, colorful serapes, large sombreros and huaraches soled with used Goodyear tires, this mixed bag of long-haired youth seemed oblivious to the

The Chowder House Marching Kazoo Band, notorious and unforgettable all at once. The lovely Bodner sisters proudly carry our banner, while "James Bond" leads the musicians dressed as Zorro, wielding his miniature garden rake like a sword. God, but we had fun this day. Photos by Esther Ditler.

FIRST PRIZE for a Comic Entry was won by Chowder House Marching Kazoo Band for the 2nd year.

Tommy Lark photos

This classic Tommy Lark photo adorned the cover of the SD Evening Tribune *the following day. How proud were we?*

Sheriff's Department Mounted Division in front of us and the pungent mess their horses were creating.

Likewise, we scarcely noticed the Model T Club behind us, steam shooting out of their radiators in the late-morning heat. The thermometer registered 103 degrees and it wasn't even 10 a.m. yet.

Suddenly the leader of this band of locals rose to his feet, adjusted his black cape and stovepipe hat, raised his baton (a miniature gardening rake) and roused his followers to their wobbly feet.

His name was Ed Galasyn, but he would eventually change it legally to "James Bond." Years later he was arrested for carrying a handgun inside of a hollowed-out Bible. He lived in his VW bus, in Pike and Jane Meade's yard, under a big tree along Star Park Circle, and seemed harmless at the time. Perhaps he was always harmless, albeit a little paranoid. But that day Ed was the magnificent Major of the Chowder House Marching Kazoo Band.

The staging area came alive with movement. The Model T cars tested their awooga horns and revved their engines. The backfires caused nearby horses to jump out of rank, refusing to respond to commands by their riders. But the Chowder House Marching Kazoo Band stood silently by, waiting for Ed to give the signal.

As we rounded the corner at First Street and Orange Avenue, the crowd that had assembled along both sides broke into cheers. The parade announcer yelled, "And here they come . . . the Chowder House . . . Marching . . . Kazooooooooo Band."

Ed raised his "baton" and, on cue, our army of musical (hung-over) "Mexican" peasants elevated our kazoos and broke into "Spanish Flea" by Herb Alpert and the Tijuana Brass.

We looked like a bunch of ugly girls.

The hair and dress regulations at Coronado High School had been lifted just two years prior. It's amazing what two years without a barber can do to a young man's appearance. We looked like a bunch of ugly girls. It was a moment to remember, even if most of those who participated in the actual band are fuzzy today in recalling details.

We, and I include myself in this wayward but dedicated lot, had hair down to the middle of our backs. We were tan from the sun and fit from surfing dawn to dusk. We were young and invulnerable, and, unbeknownst to us, we were marching through an invisible portal marking the beginning of our adult lives.

As we headed down Orange Avenue, we were exalted in response to the deafening roar of the crowd that greeted us. So much so that even those who couldn't carry a tune in practice were pitch perfect as we then broke into another of our ten-song kazoo playlist. I don't think we ever got past song number six that day.

As "Spanish Flea" ended, Tommy Harris began to whisper back through the ranks, " 'Tijuana Taxi,' 'Tijuana Taxi,' " and we began our next song. The crowd seemed to get louder and louder as we marched.

COMICS CLASSIFIED ADVERTISING

The San Diego Union WOMEN

104th YEAR   TELEPHONE 234-7111   SAN DIEGO, CALIFORNIA, WEDNESDAY MORNING, JULY 5, 1972   PAGE D-1

Balcony on Orange Avenue serves as grandstand and lunchroom for some of the 20,000 persons who watched the 25th annual Coronado Independence Day Celebration. A friend on a float, or perhaps just a funny clown, draws attention of Michelle Lund, 3.

Another, lesser-known tradition on July Fourth, was "party at Steve Anderson's place." Steve was renting the little apartment above the liquor store at Ninth and Orange. I can still identify them. From left is Bill Petrie, Coby, Mike McCartin, Bobby Murline, John and Jim Connor, and Steve Anderson. Photo by another great shooter, Bob Redding.

It was really quite the spectacle, and something none of us who were there will ever forget.

"I remember that first year very well," said Jane Meade, former owner of the Chowder House Restaurant (now called Chez Loma). "I called the guy running the parade and said I would like to have my kids' marching band in the parade. He asked who they were and I told him they were all kids who had worked with me at the Chowder House—wonderful kids, from good Navy families.

"He was wary; he wasn't sure. He knew they were a bunch of long-haired surfers. But he finally agreed to let us in. Word began to travel fast," said Jane.

"We had a policeman come into the restaurant for lunch. A friend," she said. "He mentioned he heard we were in the parade. He said he thought that would be the perfect opportunity to drop a big net over all the kids and haul them off to jail, since they were all in one place together. But he said it with a big smile."

The year before, the first year, the band wore all red, white and blue, and played songs like "76 Trombones," appropriate for the patriotic theme of the parade. Practice sessions took place regularly in Star Park leading up to the event, but no one seemed to get better. "Left, right, left . . . NO, LEFT!" Even standing motionless confused us as a group.

To all our surprise, we won first place in the Comic Division. We got a huge trophy, and Jane and Pike Meade treated all us kids to a barbecue and cold beers in back of the Chowder House."

The second year, the Chowder House Marching Kazoo Band (now with the Mexican theme) decided to take a chance and incorporate a simple dance routine into the march. When the band got in front of the judges, we performed a little roundabout dance maneuver to the song, "Tequila."

The maneuver never quite came together as a group effort, but the judges and the crowd loved it. We won first place again.

By the third year the Marching Kazoo Band was more confident. Dancing took place in the ranks and everyone put on a great show.

The theme that third year was "Bebop." By then the ranks of the Chowder House Marching Kazoo Band had swelled with little brothers and sisters and girlfriends. We took up half a city block.

Looking like a group of teenybopper/bobbysoxer high schoolers from the '50s, our group performed "Chantilly Lace" and other bopper theme songs of the era. We boys all folded cigarette packs up in our T-shirt sleeves and slicked back our hair, ala James Dean, and just did our best to look cool.

We didn't win first place that year, and were plenty mad about it. That was the year the Ocean Beach Geriatric Surf Band made its first appearance and really stole the show. Intel revealed later they got the idea for their entry from watching us the prior year.

Jane was the only adult to march in the Kazoo Band. She marched with her daughters Polly Harris, Susie and Katie Meade, sons Tommy and Joey Harris, and nieces Pam, Caroline and Bunny Haines. If I'm not mistaken, their brother, Robbie Haines, the Olympic Gold Medal sailor, also was a member of the Kazoo Band.

After the parade, it was a ritual to take over Star Park. Sometimes Nick Reynolds and his Kingston Trio performed on the front porch of Jane and Pike Meade's Wizard of Oz house. Sometimes it was Nick's nephew Joey Harris and his band, Fingers. Once, Joey played alongside another Trio member, the legendary John Stewart. We were one very large and extended family in those days. People ask what old Coronado was like? This is it. I love these people like family. We'll never see a time or place like this again in our lifetimes. Photo by Joe Ditler.

An integral member of the group was the popular Chez Loma chef, "Captain" Don Gambrill. "Big" John Atkinson brought up the rear, playing a large bass drum so we could keep some semblance of a beat amidst the deafening roar of the crowd (and the pounding of our collective hangovers).

"I remember two sisters carried the flag that first year and went braless, which all the boys just loved," said Jane. My recollection is that the Bodner sisters owned that prestigious honor. The rest of the band members mostly ranged from 13 to 19 years in age.

Of course, the occupants of "The Ghetto," a group of falling down rental houses in the middle of the island, were well represented in John Gillem and all the surfing "Bros."

> **. . . it was an important chapter
> in Coronado history.**

As a July Fourth tradition, Star Park often turned into a post-parade gathering spot for Coronado's youth. Pike and Jane Meade, owners of the "Wizard of Oz House" on Star Park Circle, were surrogate parents to most of us. Music from their front steps was an important part of the tradition, as it had been in Jane's family for generations (her brother Nick Reynolds was founding member of the Kingston Trio). Joey Harris and Fingers would perform, as well as legendary rocker John Stewart (another member of the Kingston Trio).

It was a different time, and yet it was an important chapter in Coronado history. Each generation has its favorite parade floats, special viewing area, or particular memory. Mine, obviously, is the Chowder House Marching Kazoo Band. And yet, this parade is steeped in history.

***

That first Coronado Independence Day Parade took place in 1888. The Belt Line Railroad had just been completed around the Silver Strand. The Hotel del Coronado was very close to completion and a roundhouse was being constructed at the Ferry Landing at the foot of Orange Avenue to accommodate train engines, rail cars and trolleys.

An estimated 11,000 people turned out for that inaugural parade. A contingent of 400 arrived by train from Los Angeles. The rest came, for the most part, by ferryboat. It was the 100-foot paddle wheeler Coronado.

As the only ferry in operation at that early point in Coronado's transportation history (two others, Silver Gate and Benecia, would arrive before year's end), the Coronado carried 13 horse teams and more than 600 people on her wooden decks. She ran non-stop until 11 p.m. that night. She cost $15,000 to build and was worth every penny of that investment.

Today more than 100,000 people attend the Coronado July Fourth Parade. Over the decades there have been a number of parade memories probably best left forgotten, such as spooked horses, drunken drivers (and politicians), streakers, kids playing pranks.

Late in the afternoon of July Fourth, 1888, the Hotel Del put on a daylight pyrotechnic display on the grounds. The agenda of fireworks included prismatic lights, blazing sun, caprice wheel and Roman candles.

An errant spark, however, dropped into one of the boxes and set off everything at once. Horses became frightened and bolted through the streets. People scrambled from the grounds and ran screaming in every direction. Fortunately, no one was hurt.

In 1896, celebrated architect Irving J. Gill was chairman of the Committee on Floats for the July Fourth parade.

In 1938, Central Drug Store advertised fireworks for sale. In those days it was legal to set them off anywhere in town, and selections offered included Roman candles, sparklers and pinwheels.

"Teenage Tommyrot," as the newspapers called them, could purchase dynamite blasting caps over the counter, and would attempt to blow the trolley off the tracks just for fun (some succeeded).

In 1965, 55,000 people lined Orange Avenue to see the July Fourth parade touted as "Coronado's 18th Annual." Apparently, the parade was only held sporadically in the early years.

In 1998, the July Fourth Parade Committee celebrated the 50th anniversary of the parade as an annual event. John Laing had been the parade chairman since 1970. His father, Al Laing, had been parade announcer for 40 years and was well remembered by locals for his beautiful tenor voice.

In 1998, the Lone Ranger's horse "Silver" got loose. Officials chased him all over Spreckels Park before capturing the famous white stallion.

Another time a baby elephant ran through the front yard of someone's house in the staging area. Prior to the 1970s it was a common sight to see parade horses galloping along our beach after the parade.

Actor Clint Walker (of the hit TV Western "Cheyenne") was set to ride in the parade one year but was talked out of his horse by then-mayor Robin Goodenough. The Mayor rode the horse; Clint rode in the Mayor's convertible.

In the mid-1950s the Navy Frogmen (UDT/precursor to SEALs) had a float in the parade that consisted of a huge tank of water with a "mermaid" inside. She was outfitted in a bikini top and full mermaid tail, but along the route her top was removed, much to the surprise of onlookers. The mermaid wasn't invited back, although the Navy and our Navy SEALs are featured prominently every year in the parade, and receive standing ovations, as well they deserve.

Like the subtitle of this book exclaims, "It can't happen here." And yet it did. Parade memories are among our favorites. For the Marching Kazoo Band members, it was a short-lived claim to fame but remembered nonetheless.

Just as the Bike Race veterans, Kazoo Band members (many of whom are one and the same) grew to become doctors, attorneys, politicians, pilots, writers, educators, professionals, parents and grandparents.

As all of these former Chowder House Marching Kazoo Band members, Bike Race participants, pop festival attendees, surfers and hitchhikers can attest to, Coronado provided us with our own special rite of passage and is looked back upon with no shortage of fondness.

That's my story, and I'm stickin' to it.

EPILOGUE

"How Many Summers Do You Have Left?"

Recently, in church, the Reverend Steve Mather (who has his own incredible Coronado history) was pacing back and forth in front of his congregation.

I sit in the front row of this little church, the Coronado Community Church. To illustrate just how powerful his message is, and how powerful his sermons are, we meet in the cafeteria of Village Elementary School, not a massive church with stained-glass windows, wooden pews and history, but a kids' dining hall.

We meet in the only place available to us, and we love it. More than adequate evidence, I would say, that the Message is more important than any man-contrived aesthetics.

Anyway, Mather was pacing back and forth, but when he got to me, he stopped, put his hands behind his back and leaned over like an old school teacher might have done just before scolding me.

"You," he said to me as I sat totally frozen in my chair. "Just how many summers do you have left?" Well, it wasn't appropriate to answer,

137

Tickets for *The Last Race* were created by master forger Al Sweeney, formerly of Coronado Company fame. These are collectible items today.

A typical Coronado beach cruiser – mandatory bike race equipment. Your bike and your beer mug were your most important friends on this day. Notice the high-rise handlebars, custom seat and extended seat post. With this set up, you had to be at least 6'2" to steal my bike.

Yes, surfing and Coronado have been very, very good to me. Every day, before paddling out, I drop to one knee and thank the Lord for the Blessings he has bestowed on me on this day. Photo by Donna Grace Alexander.

One of my prouder moments. We four Bros all made it into the finals of the Masters Division (old guys division). Of course, I came in last, but what righteous company I'm keeping in this photo. From left, Goob (John Gillem), Joe Dit (me), Big Al (Alec MacKenzie) and Hare (Tommy Harris). I love these guys like no others.

and I'm sure he didn't expect an answer. But ever since, that's all I can think about.

How many summers do I have left? I'm 68 this November (2019), and my parents didn't make it past 70. How many more Santa Ana conditions will I experience? How many more waves will I catch; sunsets will I gasp at? How many more times will I be able to tell my children, Jack and Chelsea, how much I love them?

Well, only the Lord knows those answers, but I think you get my drift. Enjoy every day as though it were the last. Don't fret and worry about things that haven't yet happened. And this is the big one: Remember to be grateful to your Lord. Pray and pray often. And I look forward to seeing you on the other side, where we, no doubt, will pick up this conversation once again. I'd like that . . .

Thank you, Coronado, for welcoming me from Muscoy onto the doorstep of Paradise and the Pacific. And thank you to all the wonderful people in my life who have shaped me, indulged me, loved me.

Once again, I leave these memories as someone who is grateful to have survived those years. Some would say that, in the grand scheme of things, the Summer of Love pales in comparison to other major events during the past 50 years. But these were important years, never to be recreated. They changed us; they changed society. The ripple effect continues to this day, just like that stone tossed into the pond.

When you listen to the music from those two decades, I think you'll agree, if you were there with me, it was indeed the soundtrack of our lives. Subsequent generations can read about it, can try to imagine what it was like, but, my friends, we were there.

Like a good cognac, Drambuie or Grand Marnier, if you're going to write about it, you had better know first-hand what it tastes like, what it feels like, and, most importantly, how it affected you.

God Bless.

Joe Ditler

. . . pouring my heart out in a song
Owning up for prosperity
For the whole damn world to see
Quietly now while I turn a page
Act one is over without costume change
The principal would like to leave the stage
The crowd don't understand . . .

—Rod Stewart

ACKNOWLEDGMENTS

I thank all the marvelous photographers, both professional and amateur, who contributed to the visuals in this book. We didn't have cell phone cameras in the '60s and '70s, but, as you can see, we made do with what we had and if a photo was in focus, well, you considered yourself lucky.

Thanks also to everyone who ever shared a story or adventure with me in the gathering of these memories. And how could I have done this without the incredible encouragement and ongoing love shown me from nearly 2,000 Facebook friends. Love you all! Well, almost all (smile). There are far too many of you to name, but you know who you are and I love you for that. Remember, these are your memories too. I'm just the messenger, the storyteller.

My appreciation to Dean Eckenroth Sr. and Dean Eckenroth Jr., for their support of my writing for decades. Some of these stories saw their first light of day in the pages of the Coronado Journal, Coronado Eagle and CORONADO Magazine. I've been working on and off with them for 36 years.

Thanks to Sean Elder, Lisa Bruce, Gabriel Wisdom and Ken Kramer, who risked their reputations by sharing kind words about me and my storytelling. I promise my next books will be about mainstream history, now that I've gotten this one out of my system.

Among those who kindly provided photos and visuals for my journeys through this window of Coronado history are Terry Bucklew,

Debbie (O'Toole) Riddle, Don "Woody" Woodhouse, Caroline Haines, Jim Robeson, Sue Hacker, Steve Anderson, Bruce Muirhead, Peachy Putnam, Jim Newhall, Dale Frost, Gary Kidd, Beverly Tuominen, Marty Jensen, Debbie Packard, John Gillem, Gail Hardy, Rick Tugent, Deborah Toogood-Oliver, Rex Gammon, Wayne Kaliff, April and Dean Atkinson . . . and that shadowy, unidentified Long Bar photographer somewhere across the Border, who always seemed to pop up at just the right time.

There were a precious few who worked behind the scenes with me, encouraging me, lifting my often-sagging spirits, helping me down the path toward publishing. Of the five books I could have written, it was this one my son Jack said I should lead with. Thank you, Jack, and Chelsea too, for more reasons than I can list here. I love you both dearly.

Others crucial to this process include the fabulous Joe Balla and Gary Carter. How Coronado could have existed without their presence and contributions here, I just don't know. Long live the Chart House. Long live the West Coast Ironworks.

Thanks to Jim Robeson for a lifetime of friendship and spiritual guidance. My gratitude to Donna Grace Alexander, who has never been short of opinion or inspiration, and never shy about delivering either. Thanks to the often-flawed, immensely lovable and certainly unforgettable "Bros." Surf on my brothers.

I owe a major debt of gratitude to John Freeman who jump-started me more than once on this book. John and I have been chasing deadlines (and tennis balls) for decades together.

Thank you to another veteran of the waterfront, Larry Edwards, for your editing prowess, and Tim Brittain for your terrific artwork (and enlightened patience). Thank you to fellow writer Bill Manson who trudged many paths and braved many days at sea with me in search of stories. Bill? Looks like I won this joust. As I recall, the prize is a cup of coffee at Café Madrid to the first one who finishes his book this year.

I'd also like to thank Candice Hooper (and Christian Esquevin) and the incredible Coronado Public Library. As the years pass, all of us will stumble across photos from the early days in Coronado. Or, while rummaging through your mother's things you might unearth photos of Tent City, or a Coronado from that other era. When that happens, stop! Gather them up, and make an appointment to visit the Coronado Public Library. This is the one institution, above all others, that will survive long after we are gone.

Their archivists and researchers are state-of-the-art and handpicked (and trained). It is there you will find my archives, and the thousands of historic images I've steered their way over the years; images from folks just like you. You see, it's at the Coronado Library where our history will remain safe, protected, and yet available to anyone with a library card, for generations to come. This is the ultimate destination for Coronado history.

In closing, where would this book be without the music of KPRI-FM? Thank you to the legendary DJs from KPRI and in particular Nick Schram, Ron Middag and Gabriel Wisdom. The sound of KPRI served as our musical wallpaper throughout those years. It was probably present when you lost your virginity, or went skinny dipping at Gator Beach with your high school sweetie, on a midnight ferryboat ride across the bay, or during any one of a thousand memories from this era. It was the music we fell asleep to (passed out to) and woke up to. I'm honored to weave its magic throughout the retelling of these stories.

Often, at night, just before I drift off into sleep, I think of those early DJ voices—from Wolfman Jack to Uncle Ben. I sometimes let a favorite song drift into my consciousness and just lie there and smile. I lived through it, and, by my reckoning, I've earned it. As my eyes grow heavy, I imagine I can hear the faint howling of the Wolfman. Something I'll never forget; and his unique voice saying, "Have mercy, baby. Have mercy."

CPSIA information can be obtained
at www.ICGtesting.com
Printed in the USA
BVHW042008170619
551228BV00003B/3/P